BLESS YOU
HEART ATTACK
FOR BEING IN MY LIFE

Aged 65, Bruce Wilson suffered a misdiagnosed heart attack. He was offered 50/50 odds that emergency surgery might save his life.

This gripping narrative tells of his journey to a health that literally hangs by a few threads and results uncomfortably in a new life that challenges almost everything he previously was and believed.

The most striking aspect of this unflinchingly personal self-examination is the wide-ranging collection of ideas. Augustine, Freud, Sartre, Girard to mention only a few – come together in a substantial but vivid invitation to re-examine the realities of life around and within us.

Don Meadows
Retired psychotherapist
Former editor of *The Australasian Journal of Psychotherapy*

Grounding his recent spiritual journey in ancient Christian teachings, Bruce Wilson is aware that, but for modern medical technology, his journey would have been thwarted by an early death. But avoiding death is not his focus, as he contends with heart disease, clinical complexity and determining where God is.

Those facing life-threatening situations and those seeking God in the context of 'everyday life' are offered new insights from Bishop Wilson's struggles.

Professor Bernard W. Stewart AM
Faculty of Medicine, UNSW Sydney

A heart attack – a physical, emotional but also an intellectual and spiritual journey. Bruce Wilson, telling his story from a patient's perspective, is inviting us into a bigger story. A story which can help each of us reflect on ourselves, our world, life and death. A story inviting us to reflect on experience by rediscovering some of the riches of our culture's heritage of intellectual and spiritual thought.

Bishop Genieve Mary Blackwell
Assistant Bishop in the Anglican Diocese of Melbourne

BLESS YOU HEART ATTACK FOR BEING IN MY LIFE

WRESTLING WITH DEATH, HEALTH, SELF & SPIRIT

BISHOP BRUCE WILSON

COVENTRY PRESS

Published in Australia by
Coventry Press
33 Scoresby Road
Bayswater Vic. 3153
Australia

ISBN 9780648566144

Copyright © Bruce Wilson 2019

All rights reserved. Other than for the purposes and subject to the conditions prescribed under the *Copyright Act*, no part of this publication may be reproduced, stored in a retrieval system, or transmitted in any form or by any means, electronic, mechanical, photocopying, recording or otherwise, without the prior permission of the publisher.

Scripture quotations are from the *New Revised Standard Version Bible*, copyright 1989, Division of Christian Education of the National Council of the Churches of Christ in the United States of America. Used by permission. All rights reserved.

Cataloguing-in-Publication entry is available from the National Library of Australia http:/catalogue.nla.gov.au/.

Cover design by Ian James - www.jgd.com.au
Text design by Megan Low (Filmshot Graphics FSG)

Printed in Australia

CONTENTS

Foreword
      Scott Cowdell 11

Part One
      An Unwelcome Visitor 15

Part Two
      A Welcome Visitor 77

"Bless you prison, bless you for being in my life. For there, lying upon the rotting prison straw, I came to realise that the object of life is not prosperity as we are made to believe, but the maturity of the human soul."

Aleksandr I. Solzhenitsyn, *The Gulag Archipelago 1918–1956*

Dedication

For William Meldrum-Hanna,
the surgeon with beautiful hands

Foreword

In two 1983 sermons, not long before his end, another Anglican bishop, John A. T. Robinson, issued his own dispatches from the same "valley of the shadow of death" in which Bishop Bruce Wilson found himself. For Robinson, it was terminal cancer, while for Wilson it has been a succession of life-threatening heart problems that he has remarkably survived, though physically much diminished.

While Robinson could at least give thanks for an entirely positive experience of medical treatment, Wilson tells a more complicated story. He would have avoided the damage and the resulting trauma had it not been for a botched initial diagnosis.

Both Robinson and Wilson manage to find God in their struggle with uncertainty and powerlessness, through much honest, patient and mature reflection. But where Robinson presents as a cerebral Cambridge don and reserved Englishman, Wilson brings no less an intellect while also offering a generous, no-holds barred memoir – of a shocking brush with death, of a close and loving family, of a much-cherished cat, and of finding a new breakthrough to God *in extremis*. Here we see the small story of a life on the edge made sense of in light of Christianity's "Big Story" as Wilson calls it – and vice versa.

First, it is *a story of spiritual maturity*. We learn about how God drew Wilson in via a deep experience of the frailty of our shared human condition, and hence into deeper compassion for others; about how a trusting faith actually takes root, and about how our images of God can be exploded and extended. We also see how key elements of Christian faith as set out in the Church's ancient creeds – Christ, the Holy Spirit, the Church, the life of the world to come – can spark up in new ways right at the point when so many in Australia are happy to jettison all of that. Indeed, what Wilson calls the "New Orthodoxy" of fashionable atheism emerges from his apologetic memoir as unimaginative and avoidant, compared with an adult spiritual realism that is both Christianly orthodox and genuinely liberating.

In particular, we are offered hard-won insights into what prayer most truly is, beyond immature wish fulfilment. And we are privileged to see the nature of forgiveness laid bare, as Wilson confronts and then forgives the medico who could have spared him all this suffering from the outset had he been more attentive and proactive. We learn that "forgiving and forgetting" first requires being honest about the fault, then transcending our natural tendency to seek vengeance, and finally refusing to let the future be held captive to the past. In these and other ways, Wilson invites us beyond a widespread spiritual child*ish*ness (embraced by many believers, just as it is rejected by many atheists) to a spiritual child*like*ness, showing us what it means to be what I call adult children of God.

So, second, and, as the flip side of my first point, this is *a theological story*. That is, it is "God talk". And like all trustworthy Christian God talk, it brings reason to bear in lively conversation with Scripture and the great past tradition of Christian reflection.

But here we see reason straining at the edge of incomprehensible realities, and new personal experience posing questions that had not arisen with such force for Wilson previously.

This led him to new images of God, such as a vast grey ocean on which he vividly imagined himself safely adrift, and as a lump of concrete. For me, these images recall Old Testament figures: the chaotic waters of Genesis 1 that were tamed by God's creator Spirit, and the reliable picture of God as a rock. But these impersonal slants on Christianity's "three-personed God" also resonate with certain currents of Eastern spiritual wisdom, and would prove fruitful for interreligious dialogue.

Yet despite the spiritual newness that Wilson discovers, he also arrives at a deeper appreciation of Christianity's "Big Story" that he already knew, centred as it is on Jesus Christ, his suffering, and his eventual triumph at Easter. This is a reality in which the Church still participates (for all its faults, which Wilson freely acknowledges). In the way Wilson works all this through, he provides a model for mature theological reflection. His account of the life world (indebted to the phenomenologists, and to Whitehead) forms the theological heart of his book. It illustrates the nature of Christian conviction, which is chiefly *hermeneutical* rather than uncomplicatedly *empirical* (as the atheists tend to think): that is, imagination and intellect combining with faith's traditional narratives plus lived experience to yield an account that is sufficiently compelling even if never fully certain. Wilson also explores Christianity's metaphysical confidence, through faith in God's creation, that human minds really do inhabit reality that our concepts are not at a mental remove from the "real world," as modern thought has tended to suppose, and hence we can dare to risk the adventure of trusting our instincts.

Then, third, this is *a masculine story*. Bruce Wilson is a strong, virile man – a former sprinter and footballer – yet he is deeply self-aware, and in touch with his feelings. Hence he finds himself able to frankly name and to patiently live with the loss of strength (and of libido) that is now his lot. We note throughout the priority he places on intimate male friendships, too, though certainly not of a more typically superficial sort. Today's advocates of masculine spirituality, such as the Catholic Franciscan writer Richard Rohr, would find this book to be an object lesson.

To conclude, I want to pay tribute to Bruce Wilson for the gift he has given us in these pages. Like John Robinson, who reached out to a newly sceptical generation in the 1960s with a thoughtful and honest faith – "honest to God" – so Bruce Wilson has similarly fulfilled his apostolic commission as a bishop. May many hearts be touched, burdens lifted, minds enlightened and lives changed as a result of reading this book.

Canberra
June 2019

Rev. Dr. Scott Cowdell is a Research Professor in Public and Contextual Theology at Charles Sturt University, Canberra, and Canon Theologian of the Canberra-Goulburn Anglican Diocese.

PART 1

AN UNWELCOME VISITOR

She even shaved my scrotum: for God's sake, why?

To howls of sibling protests, my sometimes outrageous brother-in-law Steve, who delights to shock conservative family members, nicknamed his newborn son 'Scrote'. After a few years he desisted, finally persuaded that this sobriquet would cause his son psychological damage.

It was approximately 8.30 pm on Saturday night April 26 2008 that a hospital nurse began to shave my 'scrote'. I knew even then that I was being changed: being transformed physically, psychologically, metaphysically and spiritually.

How we respond to major afflictions in our lives is either our making or our breaking. My purpose in telling the following story is not to focus morbidly or self-indulgently on life-threatening illness and the hazards and benefits of modern medical practice. Others have suffered much worse and more complicated afflictions than mine. But rather to explore the profound existential, spiritual, ethical and metaphysical transformations that brushes with mortality engender. With the prospect that my story may give others insight, courage and hope. It is a story about finding deeper meaning.

I suspect my story may be more of a challenge to men than to women. The former are more expert at suppressing their emotions and at avoiding psychological and spiritual challenges. But male or female, critical illness tends to batter down the ramparts of our psychological defences, throwing up great challenges to our identity, even to our very being.

RUGBY PAIN OR PLEURISY

My trouble began three weeks earlier, around 1a.m. on April 4. Except for Henry the cat, I was alone in my writing retreat at Mount Victoria in the Blue Mountains, two hour's drive west of Sydney. I awoke with excruciating shoulder pain. It was the left shoulder, the one dislocated during a try-saving tackle that, aged twenty-three, ended my inglorious rugby career. The pain was more severe than my memory of the rugby injury. I thought it might be the consequence of the joint, more than four decades later, going arthritic. It was unrelenting, hour after hour, without respite.

As soon as his medical clinic was open for the day, I called my doctor. It was his day off but, insistent with the secretary that the matter was urgent, I managed to get an appointment with a partner GP for the early afternoon. As the day wore on, the pain remained excruciating. By mid-morning, I was the pain. The pain was in me and I was in the pain – intense, a punishing psycho-physical unison of pain.

We were in the midst of juggling houses (and finance). My wife Zandra had recently retired as a bookshop manager in the central west town of Orange. A one and half hour commute north-west from Mt Victoria. I had been driving back and forth weekly for six years. The Mt Victoria retreat was for sale. The Orange cottage was already sold. We had just purchased a big house and garden at Leura – twenty minutes by car further down the mountains east of Mt Victoria, closer to Sydney – and had half moved in. Zandra was staying there overnight. I phoned her and in pain-induced tears asked her to come to Mt Vic urgently. I needed comforting. And I needed her to drive me to the doctor's rooms some twenty minutes away west at Lithgow. I was incapable of driving myself.

On our way, we passed the local hospital. Its attention-grabbing signage pointing the way to Emergency. It didn't occur to either of us to go there. We are of an age and era when you go to hospital Emergency only if you've broken a limb, been bitten by a snake or injured in a car smash. For all other matters, you go to your family doctor or, as was the case through our childhood years, your family doctor comes to you - carrying a little black bag of diagnostic tools and medicines - on a home visit. Decades of good health meant we had not kept up with changed practice. We were medical dinosaurs.

We arrived for the appointment a few minutes early. I staggered, doubled-over with pain, from the car park. This was not the usual town-fringe medical centre where occasionally I had consulted with my new, regular GP, but an alien place in the town centre. We were told the doctor would be late, delayed by patient problems at the hospital we had just driven past. Nothing relieved the unrelenting pain of the last fourteen hours.

But in that featureless and foreign waiting room I found a grain of comfort by curling-up as best I could into a foetal position.

The doctor eventually arrived, ushered us into his consulting room, briefly apologised for the delay, appeared not to notice my doubled-over contortion, and asked what the matter was. What happened next is best related in a letter of complaint I wrote in late June 2008, some two months later. (**Both the doctor's name and that of my regular GP are changed in order to preserve their privacy.**)

> *At the consultation on April 4th I advised Dr Qem that I was experiencing excruciating pain, I said '9' on a scale of '10 maximum', in my left shoulder and across that shoulder to the neck. I said that I had been doing some heavy gardening work and that in my early twenties I had dislocated that shoulder and asked whether I could have a pinched nerve or something like that. Dr Qem got me to raise my left arm high and to rotate the shoulder and said that as the pain did not change with movement he did not think that was it. I then said to him that at about my age my father had had a heart attack and his symptom was severe pain in the left shoulder. I asked Dr Qem 'Could I be having a heart attack?' He, in turn asked me 'Are you breathless?' I said 'No'. He then said 'Well you are definitely not having a heart attack'.*
>
> *Dr Qem then said several times 'It's a mystery, I'm not sure what it is'. He then said 'My best guess*

is that it's pleurisy, have you got a cough?' I replied that I did not have a cough. Dr Qem listened to my chest with a stethoscope. Dr Qem then briefly explained what pleurisy was and repeated that this was his 'best guess' diagnosis. He prescribed an antibiotic, an anti-inflammatory and a strong pain killer. I went home, took the prescribed medications, went to bed, slept for eight hours and woke free of the shoulder pain.

Though accurate on the surface, that last sentence conceals a deeper story. I did go to bed and I did indeed sleep for eight hours. But not until the strong painkiller kicked in. And not until I managed to escape from an all-encompassing fear. An existential teetering at the edge of a yawning, bottomless psycho-spiritual abyss of foreboding death. I was afraid to sleep because I feared I would never wake up again.

I was distressed, too, by realising that my will was out of date and that Zandra would be dumped alone into the mess of the unrealised sale of Mt Vic and the half-moved-into Leura house. I called her to my bedside, told her I felt that I was dying, and asked her to make sure that certain provisions in my current will would be applied differently. As I will explain, I overcame the existential foreboding and eventually got to sleep. When I woke next morning, I noticed that my urine was dark brown in colour. I had no idea what that meant but it was alarming.

I can't recall how I spent the new day. I think I just rested with a book and snoozed in front of the television. But over the next ten days or so, I tried to live normally. I managed to paint the raw timber of some folding, glass-panelled doors recently installed in the Leura house. I remember visiting the hardware store to buy the paint. I swayed from side to side, stumbling with dizziness, as I walked from the car park. I arrived home with two cans, each holding two litres of paint. Half a litre would have been more than enough for the whole job. (An unopened two litre can remains on a shelf in my garage to this day.) I couldn't paint standing so had to arrange seating at various heights. Even so, I could work for only about thirty minutes at a time without complete exhaustion. I felt ghastly.

Located on the spine of the Blue Mountains, Leura is an up and down, steep, hilly region. More so around our new house which is in a little valley. (My daughter is married to a New Zealander and his family's gratuitous advice is that the Blue Mountains should be renamed the 'Blue Hills' because they can't see anything a New Zealander would call a mountain.) Due to the hilly nature of the region, back then mobile phone signals were non-existent. They are intermittent still today. Zandra had flown to Melbourne to attend a family funeral, staying overnight. To check on her welfare, I struggled slowly up a nearby hill in search of a signal to phone her. Breathless, at the top of the hill, I tested my pulse rate. It was 145. After the call, and as I walked effortlessly down the hill, I tested it again. It was 145. The same when I arrived home. Even after sitting for a while, it was still 145. In bed later that night, it stayed at 145. This was odd and alarming.

I don't now recall how I explained these things to myself. Nor how I explained why my substantial capacity for physical work – such as sweeping autumn leaves from our driveway – was now limited to about twenty minutes. Or why, two days later at his house, assisting my son-in-law Kevin to assemble some pre-fab furniture, left me exhausted beyond measure. O.K. I admit it was Ikea – with impossible to follow instructions – but even that could not explain my extreme fatigue. At the time, I think I put it down to the effects of pleurisy or to the side effects of the drugs prescribed to counter it. My memory now is vague but, written soon after, the complaint letter against the doctor is pretty clear:

> I continued taking the antibiotic and the anti-inflammatory. But the next seventeen days of my life were what I can only describe as 'weird'. I went to bed early each night, much more tired than usual, felt the cold in a way I had never previously felt it, had a racing and sometimes irregular heartbeat, got a bit dizzy at various times during the day, my eyes went 'funny' on a couple of occasions, I had hot flushes and felt panicky, sometimes all day. But I also went about the normal day to day things I do.
>
> My daughter has been subject to panic attacks in the past and she, my wife and I put down my symptoms to such attacks. (As a result of Dr Qem's strong assertion to the negative, it did not occur to me that I may be suffering post heart attack symptoms.)

Almost three weeks later, after I'd recovered from the intensity of that scary night and day of excruciating 'pleurisy' pain, the course of prescribed antibiotics now completed, I was still most unwell. So it was time to visit the doctor again. This time to my fairly new, but regular GP.

A BIT ABOUT ME

In mid 2000, I took early retirement from my position as bishop of the Anglican Diocese of Bathurst. My home and office were in Bathurst, home to Australia's greatest car race and to my diocese's cathedral – 200 kilometres west from Sydney. But the diocese itself takes in nearly a third of the State of New South Wales. All of the Central West up to the Queensland border, an area approximately 700 by 350 kilometres. Visiting churches and clergy in the cities and towns of this vast territory, I was driving about 65,000 kilometres a year. I calculated that since my election over ten years earlier, I had personally driven the equivalent of a trip to the moon and back. I had been a bishop (first in Canberra) for 16 years in total and was pretty much physically and psychically burnt out. As mentioned, Zandra continued her job as a bookshop manager in Orange, 45 minutes north-west of Bathurst.

After resigning, for the next six years, I spent half my week in Orange and half at the Mount Victoria writing retreat. (Mt Vic was my official address as it's considered professionally unethical – *infra dig* – for a retired bishop to reside in his former diocese; keeping out of the new bishop's way.) My Siamese Oriental cat 'Henry' was my constant companion at both places. And at both places I saw 'customers' – I could never find the right word – for a new ministry I began of one-on-one, face-to-face psycho-spiritual guidance for senior clergy and bishops. I also commissioned, edited - and myself wrote articles for - the privately and independently owned national Anglican newspaper *Market Place*.

GP VISIT

As with all my previous life, in these years I had little need for, and seldom consulted, a medical doctor. I did consult a GP in Orange a couple of times. He prescribed medication for an acidic stomach and for slightly elevated blood pressure. So when Zandra retired in 2007, and for a planned brief period when we moved into the Mount Victoria retreat, I needed to find a new doctor just to keep up with pharmacy scripts.

Either I have been very unlucky with doctors or the profession has a large number of non-empathic or semi-competent practitioners. (Just like the clergy do I hear you say!) Because in all my years – I am 76 as I write this – I've had confidence in only two GPs: one in my early twenties and Andrew Masterton who became my new GP in 2007. The earlier one – in my twenties – diagnosed 'Jewish mother troubles' as the cause of frequent tummy and respiratory conditions. Correctly prescribing maternal separation – psychological not physical – as the effective remedy. Masterton is the one who was off duty the day I had my 16 hours of 'pleurisy' agony in April 2008. From our first consultation, I was impressed by his professional intelligence but above all by his empathy, his down to earth listening skills and a complete absence of pretension to superiority. This is why, still to this day, I travel 80 plus kilometres return from Leura to consult with him as my GP.

I informed Andrew of my visit to his colleague nearly three weeks earlier, about the symptoms I had back then, about my ongoing symptoms. And also about the family panic-attack theory to explain them. From scribbled back-of-the-envelope notes I penned for this consultation – recently rediscovered in an old file – I asked him 'am I suffering from hypochondria?' My 'closer-to-the-time' complaint letter tells what happened next.

> When I saw my own GP on April 22nd he, too, as I told him the full story from the day I saw his colleague Dr Qem, was at first inclined to think I was experiencing panic attacks and asked if I'd like a referral to a psychiatrist. But my own GP also referred me for a stress test, some blood tests and an immediate ECG examination carried out by the practice nurse. After viewing the print out of the latter he sent me immediately to the emergency department of Lithgow hospital, telling me that I had some irregular heart rhythms.
>
> Later that day (April 22) I was informed by a Lithgow hospital doctor that I had recently had a 'completed heart attack', and later still that day I was transferred by ambulance to Westmead hospital in Sydney.

There my son Richard, who lives in Sydney, caringly waited to support me.

A BIT MORE ABOUT ME AND MY THINKING

My April 4th 2008 bedtime foreboding – a sense of teetering on the edge of a metaphysical abyss – is described frequently by heart attack survivors as a threat of impending doom. Before explaining how I overcame this extreme level of anxiety – especially the fear of never waking up again – and finally got to sleep that night, a bit more relevant background about me and my thinking. Especially about spirituality, life and death.

The churches, some more than others, and their leaders, are on the nose in Australia for sins and crimes committed by clergy, especially against children in their care. As a reader, knowing I am a retired Anglican bishop, it's possible you have me stereotyped. Stereotyped as a person who is religious rather than spiritual. A person who accepts beliefs about life and the universe by blind faith without reason. A morally judgmental person who lacks compassion. A person who is sexually obsessed or repressed, or both.

Am I being defensive? Confessedly – yes! Because I know in the minds of a large number of Baby Boomer and of Gen X and Gen Y (Millennial) Australians, I am, according to this stereotype, pejoratively a 'Christian'. I certainly bear the shame of those who by their lives and actions have created this stereotype. It's a blasphemy against the life and spirit of Jesus Christ. But I hope you may look beyond, not overlook, of course, what these evil, criminal exploiters have created. They have befouled and profaned the life and work of Jesus Christ and all those saints through the centuries and today who are his faithful followers.

Can God Survive in Australia? is the title of a minor best-seller I wrote way back in 1982. It explored the waves of secularism building up in this country during the 1960s and 1970s. Waves eroding traditional religion, spirituality and metaphysics (i.e. phenomena beyond or behind the physical, sometimes crudely termed 'the supernatural').

These cultural 'Bondi rollers' created a new and purely secular way of living and believing as an Australian. A living and believing **as if** the world of everyday life, along with the science-modelled world of space-time-energy, **are, were, and forever shall be, all that there is.** A cultural-conditioning that unsights us to the infinite richness and complexity of the Lifeworld*. Waves mightily powered by winds of unparalleled economic prosperity and consumerism. Of the latter, a friend once said 'Australians aren't interested in heaven, they've got it already'.

(*Lifeworld – see shaded box at end of Part One.)

A third of a century later, these secularist, cultural waves have become a tsunami. Among high-flying opinion makers – journalists, academics, science popularisers, consumer marketeers – it is now conforming and conventional, even a bit of a badge of honour, to call oneself an atheist. Much as fifty years ago - Australia's **Old Orthodoxy** – it was conforming and conventional to call oneself Catholic, or Church of England, or Protestant. For example, Peter FitzSimons, journalist, author, broadcaster, former national rugby champion and leader of Australia's Republican Movement, whose writing I admire and enjoy, heads his twitter account 'Author, Atheist, Republican'.

FitzSimons and other older members of this **New Orthodoxy** still seem to think it's a bit daring and rebellious to be an atheist. They don't realise it's now the 21st century equivalent to 20th century ticking the 'Church of England' box on the Census form. In reality, nowadays claiming atheism is about as daringly individualistic as getting tattooed, ticking the 'no religion' box on the Census form or having avocado for breakfast. That is why I call it the New Orthodoxy.

The New Orthodoxy is so confident about itself that its critics – myself included – dub it 'the posture of knowingness'. It preaches a secularist dogma matched only in stridency and mindlessness by Christian or Islamic fundamentalists. As the philosopher Andrew Gleeson puts it: '...*knowingness includes an impatient confidence that there is nothing in the world – especially not in history or tradition, or in art and (horror) myth and religion - that a mind with a razor sharp logical training, abetted by empirical science, cannot, in principle, comprehend and judge, or could, with enough time, resources and so on'.*

The New Orthodoxy is dogmatically confident that death means oblivion. Imagined soothingly as eternal sleep, rather than empty nothingness. It holds no Shakespearean doubt, fear or pause. Not asking – '*in that sleep of death what dreams may come, when we have shuffled off this mortal coil'*. Any notion of a positively pleasant hereafter (heaven) is mocked as wishful thinking created from fear of death. Any possibility of an unpleasant hereafter (hell) is ridiculed as religious fear mongering. As a priestly control mechanism. Weirdly, people no longer die, they **pass**, but no one seems to know what this latest euphemism means. Pass to what? Where?

Though he had no pretensions to being a deep thinker, atheism was the world of my dear, deceased father. An atheist ahead of his time. But not strident. Thus atheism was the family world of my childhood and youth. A world I found empty, dreary and shallow – a psychological and spiritual desert. A world eventually I rejected to embrace the metaphysical and spiritual world that I call the 'Christian Big Story'. The story that begins at the dawn of human stories. That begins with human self-consciousness, the start of history.

Integrating my own little story into the Big Story is what I mean when I call myself a Christian. A traditional, orthodox - but definitely not a fundamentalist – Christian. It's a Big Story about fullness not emptiness, about hope not despair. Above all, it's a story about love – a trust that the world ends neither with a bang nor a whimper, but in the ecstasy of Divine love.

HEART NOT MIND PRAYER

On the night of my heart attack, I got to sleep by praying the Jesus Prayer – *'Lord Jesus Christ, Son of God, have mercy on me, a sinner'*. From the Eastern Orthodox churches. Among them known as the Prayer of the Heart. 'Heart' not, of course, meaning 'blood pump' but the centre of feeling – the core of the self. A psycho-spiritual heart: which is the usual meaning of 'heart' in the Bible. Common still in day-to-day English usage. From my theological studies, I had known – and occasionally used – this prayer for a long time. Never until this night did it possess such depth of meaning and feeling.

The Jesus Prayer is at the centre of Eastern Christianity. Its spiritual practice goes back at least as far as the Egyptian Desert Fathers of the 400s. The Eastern or Orthodox Church (think, for example, Coptic, or Greek or Russian or Serbian 'Orthodox') separated from the Western Church (think Roman Catholic, Protestant, Anglican or Pentecostal) in the 11th century. Sadly, many Australians are only aware of Western Christianity. It tends to stress belief in positive teachings about God (cataphatic theology – dogma). Eastern Orthodoxy tends to stress the unknowable otherness of God (apophatic theology– mystery). With emphasis on experience – mystical meditation and worship. These are critical differences but more of emphasis than essence. Both East and West are part of the same Christian Big Story.

That dread-full night when I went to sleep praying the Jesus Prayer, I followed the ancient practice of breathing in with the words '*Lord Jesus Christ, Son of God*' and breathing out with the words '*have mercy on me, a sinner*'. It's a prayer you pray over and over, similar to meditative mantras known in various other spiritual practices. The totality and wholeness is important – the breathing, the repetitive sound, the rhythm and the meaning of the words.

Anyone familiar only with Petitionary Prayer (prayers asking God *for* things or *to do* things) – or with secularist ridiculing notions of prayer as attempts at magical manipulation, what Freud called 'wish fulfilment' – may find it difficult to understand that the Jesus Prayer is part of what the East calls Hesychasm. Roughly meaning 'to keep stillness'. This is a practice of inner prayer, seeking union with God at a level beyond images, concepts and language. Which is why it is a prayer of the heart, not the mind. It's a prayer of knowing God through love not through reason, through heart not mind. A prayer of 'letting go' – not grasping at 'control'.

The Jesus Prayer seeks mystical union with God. Union as relationship, not absorption or oblivion. A self that God is in. And a self that is in God. Patrick White, Australia's literary Nobel laureate, says that one cannot accept God until one accepts necessity. And this night, a new and powerful necessity bound itself upon me. A heart attack necessity: more binding than anything I had previously experienced. I was beginning to learn new depths about what it means to accept God

As I lay in that hospital bed, thanks to the Jesus Prayer, I sensed that God was both in heaven and in me – closer than my own breath. Being of my being. I fell asleep as an old Methodist preacher - heard frequently on a Sydney radio station of my youth - would in simple metaphor put it – 'safe in the Everlasting Arms'.

The initial subtitle I gave this book was *Finding deeper meaning*. Occasionally, 'finding deeper meaning' creates a need to explain or to expand upon a therapeutic procedure or a slightly difficult subject. 'A Little Bit About God' is an example of the latter. If you don't want the story interrupted you can completely skip these explanations and expansions – printed in shaded boxes - or come back to them later.

A Little Bit About God

It is a serious, category mistake to seek to 'locate' God in the 'out there' world of the material universe. A mistake recognised centuries ago but perpetuated today by people who imagine they are making a scientific stand against theistic superstition.

More than 1500 years ago, recalling his adult spiritual and intellectual quest, Augustine – Professor of Rhetoric in Milan, later the Bishop of Hippo, and one of the greatest minds in Western culture – stated this clearly:

'But what is my God? I put the question to the earth. It answered 'I am not God', and all things on earth declared the same. I asked the sea and the chasms of the deep and the living things that creep in them, but they answered, 'We are not your God. Seek what is above us.' I spoke to the winds that blow, and the whole air and all that lives in it replied '…I am not God.' I asked the sky, the sun, the moon, and the stars, but they told me, 'Neither are we the God whom you seek'.

For Augustine, God is the ground of being. God is not another being among other beings. Another thing among all other things. God is Being in which all beings have their being.

The current, popular Western idea that we can discover God – much as we might discover a new planet or galaxy – is based on the absurd idea that God is a being somewhere in the outer part (to us) of the Lifeworld that God created. If being a 'believer' means believing in a God 'up there' somewhere, or 'out there' somewhere, then both Augustine and I are atheists. From my own experience – and if you think about the disparity between a Creator and a creature how could it be otherwise? – it is God who 'discovers' (or discloses) God to us. Not we who discover God. It is only up to us to be ready to respond to God with awe, trust and service.

For Augustine, Reason and Self-Consciousness are primary ways God relates to us, Spirit to spirit. In crude terms, God is an 'inner-beyond' not an 'outer-beyond'.

Our rational self-consciousness – this transcendent self – explorer of galaxies, bosons and neurons, in degree uniquely human - was for Augustine (and for me lying in a hospital ward in 2008) a primary dimension for knowing God. Spirit-to-spirit, as we might say today, or Soul-to-soul to use Augustine's terminology (realising he meant nothing material by this word):

> *'... truth says to me, 'Your God is not heaven or earth or any kind of bodily thing' ... And I know that my soul is the better part of me, because it animates my whole body. It gives it life, and this is something that no body can give to another body. But God is even more. He is the Life of the life of my soul. What do I love then when I love God? Who is this Being who is so far above my soul? If I am to reach him, it must be through my soul.'*

HOSPITAL

I drove my own car to the GP clinic and then to the hospital. Having spent the three weeks since my heart attack painting doors, climbing hills and doing all the usual domestic chores – it seemed odd that the regional hospital insisted I be transported the ninety-minute journey to Westmead lying flat on my back under an oxygen mask in an ambulance. For a person who – psychologically at least, if not rationally and intellectually – always sees himself as being in control, this was just the beginning of major transformations of consciousness. With a lot more metamorphoses around the corner. I doubt that it's just a masculine thing, but later, via hospital heart rehab, I discovered that, like me, male heart attack victims react more anxiously to the psychical loss of control than to the actual physical effects of heart troubles.

Memory of my transfer from the ambulance to the Emergency Department on the evening of Tuesday April 23, 2008 is a blur. I spent the next day in a Cardiac Ward. That too is a blur, except for the distressing spectacle of a woman in the bed next to me being emergency-team-resuscitated when her heart stopped. I cannot recall, but presumably at some time on this day, I signed the 'informed consent' forms accepting the risks of undergoing an angiogram, and possible angioplasty, scheduled for the next day. Both terms were new and meant nothing to me.

Andrew my GP jokes that 'informed consent' means that the doctor informs the patient and the patient consents to what he says. It was pretty much exactly like that. I did know that people – though personally limited in my actual experience to just one near friend – had balloon stents inserted into their hearts to open up blockages. But that was about all I knew. I could not have explained the meaning of 'angiogram' or 'angioplasty', let alone the difference between them. So much for my consent being informed!

What I did know was that on Christmas Eve 1956 my maternal grandfather died, aged 63, from his second heart attack that same year. Back then there were no effective treatments for heart attack victims. Certainly, there were no surgical or soft interventionist procedures. Heart bypass surgery, angiography and angioplasty, which Australians now taken for granted, are recent inventions that save and prolong the lives of thousands.

Angiography and Angioplasty

In essence, angiography was invented way back in 1927 by Egas Moniz, a Portuguese physician and neurologist. In 1953, Sven-Ivar Seldinger, a Swedish radiologist, invented a technique that greatly increased the safety of the procedure and in 1958 an American physician, Mason Somes, discovered the technique could be used to examine the heart's arteries. In simple terms, an angiography is an imaging procedure where a catheter (think thin, flexible wire) is threaded via an artery or vein, through the arm or groin, up into the heart, discharging a contrast substance enabling x-ray pictures to be taken of the heart's arteries. An angiogram is able to reveal artery blockages that cause a heart attack but cannot do anything about them. It is not itself a treatment.

Treatment came much later in 1964 when Charles Dotter, a US radiologist, invented angioplasty. Using this stenting technique, he saved the life of a woman with a gangrenous leg – the result of a blocked femoral artery – who had refused amputation. In 1977, Andreas Gruentzig, a German cardiologist, was the first to apply balloon angioplasty to the arteries of an awake heart patient. Today angioplasty sees the patient administered a mild relaxant, the catheter is then inserted and used to place a balloon at the point of arterial blockage, the balloon is inflated to open the blocked artery and usually a metal stent is inserted to keep the expansion open. Such extraordinary advances in such a short time-span!

I was wheeled on a trolley into the Cath Lab and the doctor who performed the angiogram and angioplasty introduced himself. He had red hair but I did not catch his name. Except for a pleasant floating sensation, the kind that comes with a little but not too much Scotch whisky, I recall just one thing. It was a resonant, rather deep, cultured male voice. I could not see either the person or the place from whence it came. It was giving instructions to the red-haired doctor. I probably would not have remembered that voice or anything it said had it not at one point been shouting with consternation 'no, no further, no further'. Those words did not disturb my relaxed floating consciousness until they came back to haunt me some days later.

The official medical report of my angiogram and angioplasty reads:

'*A coronary angiogram demonstrated a dominant right coronary artery with a 90% lesion which was stented with two overlapping bare metal stents.*' This lesion – blockage in lay terms – caused my heart attack as it prevented adequate blood flow to the heart muscle.

Next day, in the cardiac recovery ward, my default cardiologist, Lloyd Davis, came in the late afternoon to see me. (Default because like most heart attack victims I was admitted by ambulance as an emergency patient. With the wisdom of hindsight - after a medical friend 'researched him' - such was Davis' professional standing, I would happily have chosen him anyway.)

Lloyd Davis said that the angioplasty had gone well, that I should give up smoking those little cigars – which I did from that day to this – and that I could sign out of the hospital and go home tomorrow - Saturday. With joyous anticipation, I experienced the usual relief of once again becoming a person not a patient. A subject not an object. Of being well, not sick. What a contrast those words 'home' and 'hospital' connote!

Twice in the middle of that Friday night, the eve of returning home, nurses came rushing to my bed anxiously asking - 'Are you all right, Mr Wilson?'- Are you all right, Mr Wilson?' So far as I was concerned, I was perfectly all right. Disturbed only - especially with the second interruption – by being abruptly awakened. Unnecessarily, I thought, by anxiously over-solicitous carers. Next morning, a ward doctor visited. He said that my heart monitor had recorded dangerous arrhythmias during the night and that instead of being discharged I was to be moved into the cardiac observation ward.

A FELLOW COMES

Westmead hospital in Sydney's west, I discovered later that day, enjoys an international reputation for excellence in heart medicine and surgery. I learnt this from an advanced trainee cardiologist who had come from Edinburgh in Scotland to complete his specialist qualification. I wrote about his important role in the events of my heart troubles some time later. I will explain.

Dr John England became my ongoing cardiologist. His consulting rooms are at Katoomba next to Leura. John invited me to write a chapter for his book **Kickstart** (published 2011). He himself has depended on an implanted heart pacemaker for decades. Just recently, he's had valve replacement surgery. He is a rather saintly, quite eccentric man, of whom I am most fond. He has an insider's empathy with the fears of his patients. His book is subtitled: ***Everything you need to know about living with a pacemaker or defibrillator.*** Using tabloid-style language, simple structure and witty cartoons, the book aims to help heart patients understand their illness and its treatments. Part of my chapter – written just eighteen months after aneurysm surgery – continues the story of this present book. Please remember it's the Saturday when I was meant to go home. Instead, I am in the cardiac observation ward:

> Later that same morning I was told the cardiac fellow would be coming to see me. No one is better at mysterious names, not even philosophers or theologians, than doctors and hospitals. This one had me quite bamboozled. 'Cardiac' - yes that's reasonably easy, something to do with the heart. But 'cardiac fellow'? What could that mean? 'Fellow' – a male, a gent, a bloke? My best thought was – 'someone who knows something about hearts and who is not a sheila is coming to see me.' Utter mystery!
>
> Eventually, a delightful, young, and yes a 'he', doctor on secondment from Edinburgh, with a heavy Scottish accent, turned up with an enormous machine in tow. I later found out the machine is called an echocardiograph. He explained that he was at Westmead to learn from the internationally acclaimed expertise the hospital staff has in cardiology. Being a 'fellow', he said, is a fancy way of saying he is higher on the ladder of medical proficiency than a Cardiac Registrar (another funny name but let's not go there now) but not yet as high as a specialist Cardiologist.

The Fellow (a capital 'F' is correct) rubbed some gooey stuff on my chest, proceeding then to roll a ball attached by cord to the machine all over it, stopping in several places where he pressed hard but not uncomfortably. After quite a while, I saw him go pale. He called in the Cardiologist on duty that day and they chatted **sotto voce***. I got very scared but they did not explain anything. To this day, I could kick myself for not asking what was wrong. Presumably they thought their silence was sparing me from anxiety, but it was quite the opposite. They left, saying they would ask a surgeon to come and see me. By this time, I was so nervous I didn't even try to put two and two together, I just blotted out any negative thoughts.*

Zandra was present when the Fellow – Alister Rider is the name she wrote in her diary – went white in the face. Serendipitously, I owe my life to this Fellow from Edinburgh. Just as I already owed my life to my immigrant, paternal great grandparents who had come from Edinburgh to Australia in the 1850s. While Dr Rider was examining me, I felt – rather superstitiously I must confess – a sense of assurance from his heavy Edinburgh accent. His obvious alarm at whatever his machine had revealed dispelled that assurance.

Wikipedia tells me that there are three rare but dangerous complications that can arise from angioplasty. These may have been explained in the 'informed consent' form I signed, I do not know. But none of them – embolisation, arterial rupture, pseudo-aneurysm – would have meant anything but medical mumbo-jumbo to me at the time. Dr Rider's portable echocardiogram machine showed, he thought, as confirmed by his supervisor, that I was suffering from one of these three rare but dangerous complications. A pseudo-aneurysm. My **Kickstart** chapter continues the story:

> It was visiting hours and my family was all round the bed when the young (aren't they all when you get to my age?) male surgeon arrived dressed in a T shirt and jeans. It was a Saturday afternoon and I guessed he must have come from some kind of sporting activity. He said I had a pseudo-aneurysm of the heart wall. It sounded serious for sure. Though I had no idea what it meant. 'Pseudo' was a word I knew meant 'fake' or 'sham' so, for example, a pseudo-intellectual did not mean 'clever', it meant 'smart arse'. So, I thought, a pseudo-aneurysm couldn't be as serious as an authentic, real aneurysm.
>
> The young surgeon said it meant that there was a hole in the wall of my heart, that my heart was only being held together by blood clots and the thin sac (I later learnt it's called the 'pericardium') around the heart. 'Unless the aneurysm is repaired, then sometime in the next 48 hours,' he said, 'it will burst open and immediately kill you.' It was agreed that I would have urgent surgery at 7.30 the next morning. I felt very humbled that a team of highly skilled people would come to the hospital early on

the Sunday of the Anzac holiday weekend to try to save my life.

Whew! Whammy! These heart problems come at you from nowhere, at least that's how it feels.

I asked the young surgeon about the dangers of the operation and the chances of me surviving the surgery. 'About 50-50, but we don't like losing people,' he answered. He then explained that he was the assistant surgeon and that a more senior man 'who has beautiful hands' would do the main job.

Beautiful hands! Beautiful hands! No doubt an admiring image for a young surgeon impressed by the skills of his mentor! But an horrific image for a patient picturing his life-ticker being extracted bloodily from its chest cavity in a surgeon's grasp. One thing I like to tell doctors as a result of my heart troubles and treatments is that they must watch their words. The things they say with all good intentions are often either totally mysterious or completely frightening to their patients.

CHOICES

So! The options were:

A. with no surgery - a 100% chance of being dead within 24-48 hours, rammed home by the instruction 'lie in bed as still as possible, no toilet visits, pan only when necessary';

B. with surgery - a 50% chance of surviving the pseudo-aneurysm or, as a pessimist might say, a one in two chance of dying on the operating table or later in ICU.

But was there a choice? Did I choose? These were not questions I asked myself on that fateful Saturday afternoon. With my family and other intimates at my bedside it seemed to me – and to them – that there was no choice. I don't believe the young surgeon thought there was any choice either. But I can't imagine many other circumstances than 50-50 surgery that so starkly epitomise how we become our choices.

Jean-Paul Sartre, the French existentialist philosopher I studied as a young undergraduate, would insist not only that I had a choice but that to be authentic as a person (a subject) - and not to treat myself inauthentically as a mere thing without choice (an object) - I should have been conscious of making a free decision 'surgery yes' or 'surgery no', 'life yes' or 'life no'. Existentialism holds that pretending you do not have a choice is to be a thing not a person.

The fact that I am writing these words many years after 'that fateful Saturday' demonstrates that the choice was made for life-giving surgery not death. So now an essential part of what I am - my identity - is being a member of the 'zipper club'. Someone whose long, vertical chest scar with stitches is evidence of being a survivor of open-heart surgery. But did I choose or was it the case that others chose for me?

According to Sartre, when we pretend to ourselves that we have no choice we are guilty of *mauvaise foi* – bad faith. Sartre has a few well-known examples of 'bad faith'. One is of a woman on a first date. She has the choice of allowing her date to hold her hand or not. To accept or to reject his advance. But she dissociates from her hand and treats it as a thing. Not part of her. So that when the date takes her hand - or so she pretends to herself – she has not made a commitment of any kind. This for Sartre, and for the existentialist in me, is *mauvaise foi* – being inauthentic.

I concede that there is a huge difference between choosing to hold hands – or not – with a new date and choosing between life-saving surgery and death. But I'm not sure I really did choose on that fateful Saturday. This became disturbingly apparent to me some time afterwards. At home in the early days of recovery, a psychiatrist friend visited and asked me exactly the question 'Did you choose to have the invasive surgery?' Perhaps eccentrically, I was to be deeply troubled by this question long after the surgery. It became a spiritual question.

GOODBYES

Thanks to Zandra's diary, I know that the name of the young surgeon wearing T- shirt and jeans was Dr Bill Lyons. His words about not liking to lose people were not reassuring enough to exorcise the fear of a 50-50 chance of dying. So I had an overwhelming sense of need to say goodbye. By late that afternoon all my family and intimate friends had come to visit. We tearfully hugged and kissed in what we all knew could be a last goodbye. (Zandra and my daughter Anthea returned later to say 'goodnight' after 'the shave'. They had booked a hospital, visitors' room for the night.)

I was given a 'phone and called my closest male friend Don. We had become friends 47 years previously, aged 17 and 18 respectively, when he was a Med and I an Arts student at Sydney University. He had since moved to Melbourne where he now practised as a psychotherapist. My phone call was a bolt from the blue. He had no idea that I was ill, let alone in hospital. Choking with tears, I managed briefly to explain the situation and to say 'goodbye'. Weeks later, I apologised for the shock I had caused him. He was very understanding.

After the phone call, I became pretty much emotionally inconsolable about the lack of opportunity to say goodbye to Tom, my 4-year-old grandson. My other two grandchildren were just little babies but Tom and I had deeply bonded already. We both loved discovering 'treasures' – unusual animal bones, leaves or gumnuts – to bring home from our bushwalks. And we would laugh ourselves silly playing imaginary pizza store. As we topped our pizza base with all kinds of disgusting, smelly stuff.

It may perhaps be difficult to understand, but I was equally inconsolable about being unable to say goodbye to Henry my cat. Family and friends frequently described our relationship as 'joined at the hip'. I did not expect spiritual insight to appear for me from a cat, but Henry had revealed new depths of God to me.

Tolling of the bell at death's door certainly rings the changes about those things that really matter in life. A cat!

FELINE EPIPHANY

To my distress, Henry died very recently. He was a Siamese Oriental. I once calculated that he responded to over thirty English words. From 'Do you want to go outside?' to 'Do you want a rub?' He played fetch like a dog. With Henry at the top of a flight of stairs and me at the bottom, he would catch in his mouth a tightly rolled-up sock that I threw up to him. Then accurately flick it back down to me, over and over. Even on cold, wintry Blue Mountain's days, he preferred my lap to the rug in front of the slow-combustion, wood fire. When I spoke to him, he made and kept eye contact. I called him the 'cat person'.

Relationally, it was like having an athletic eighteen-month old human baby in the house After I retired from my busy life as a bishop – endlessly involved with people face to face or by phone – I found myself spending several days each week alone. Henry was my only constant companion. He travelled with me in the car from Orange to Mount Victoria and back each week.

Animal Friends

Friendship and communion with non-human creatures is not often celebrated in literature and is sometimes scorned by Western intellectuals as sentimental. There are notable exceptions. In 1801-2 Captain Matthew Flinders, along with an Aboriginal man Bungaree, was the first person to circumnavigate and map the island continent of Australia. Trim, his cat, accompanied him on the voyage. There is a statue of Trim on a window ledge at Sydney's Mitchell Library, the repository of much of Australia's early colonial records and papers. After Trim's death, Flinders penned the following tribute:

The best and most illustrious of his race
The most affectionate of friends,
faithful of servants,
and best of creatures
He made the tour of the globe, and a voyage to Australia,

*which he circumnavigated, and was ever the
delight and pleasure of his fellow voyagers*

As a parish priest, I was often asked by grieving pet lovers if dogs and cats go to Heaven when they die. No one ever asked me about a cat or a dog Hell. (The former might be on the wish list of native-animal conservationists, and the latter on that of neighbours driven mad by interminable barking.)

The death of a cat or dog may appear trivial. But in the Christian Big Story, death itself (human, cat, dog, rabbit, giraffe or snake) – the archetype of nothingness – is the deepest abyss of the fallen world we all inhabit. The New Testament names death 'the last enemy'. My enemy, our enemy and God's enemy. This enemy, it says, is not defeated by 'going to heaven' but by Heaven coming to earth. By God, in God's time, bringing into being a transformed, transfigured, unfallen 'New Creation'. Envisaged in Jesus' well-known Lord's Prayer – 'Thy kingdom come, Thy will be done in earth as it is in heaven.' Hard as it is to imagine, 'The-Age-To-Come' (heaven) is earth new-created, unfallen. The Lifeworld freed from futility, freed from pain and death. The Lifeworld freed, not just the 'human world'!

Henry made me illuminatively conscious that God loves all creatures. As Jesus says in his famous Sermon on the Mount: *'Are not two sparrows sold for a cent? Yet not one of them will fall to the ground apart from your Father.'* Henry made me aware that we humans – with our anthropocentric selfishness – are the cruellest of all earthly creatures. So 'yes', thanks to Henry, I am more than a bit of an Animal Libber these days and have an acute interest in the theology and ethics of our relationships with non-human animals. (Whatever else we may consider ourselves to be, we humans are animals too. The nature of the continuum may be contentious, but not the actual continuum.)

I wince when I hear people say of a terrorist torturer, a cruel murderer, or an evil rapist –'He behaved like an animal'. No other animal can match the cruelty of the human animal. The correct description for such unmatched evil is demonic, not animal – 'He behaved like a demon'. Only human animals take evil to a spiritual level.

In hospital, being unable to bid Henry a final goodbye was emotional agony. Since then, I have experienced the pain of saying goodbye to him as he died in my lap. I cherish the memory of prayerfully dedicating his little feline being to God as we buried his body in one of his favourite spots in our Leura garden. I guess if I had been the one first to die, he would have fretted for me. But not, I expect, with such desolate pains of loss that befall self-reflecting human animals like us. Back to Westmead hospital.

At about 7.30 pm, after I'd eaten a couple of typical hospital sandwiches, a female nurse arrived bedside saying she had to shave me in preparation for surgery next morning. I am – to quote from the biblical story of Jacob and Esau, grandsons of Abraham, revered patriarch to Jews, Christians and Muslims – 'a hairy man' like Esau. He's the brother whom Jacob deceitfully betrayed using goat's hair. I expected that my chest - to be surgically opened in order to expose my heart - would be shaved. But I did not expect a whole-body shave – from neck to toe – let alone that that would include, as I have mentioned with horror already, my scrotum.

My angiogram revealed that along with the 90% blockage in the artery that caused my heart attack, other arteries had up to 50% blockages. From the nurse about to shave me, I learnt for the first time that, as well as patching-up the pseudo-aneurysm, the surgeon with 'beautiful hands' planned to perform a couple of coronary bypasses too. (This explained why, earlier, another nurse asked if I wanted to view a video with details about open-heart surgery so that I knew what was going to happen to me. I recoiled in horror from this. No doubt a well-intentioned but insensitive proposal. Though maybe that nurse had no idea I was not a normal bypass patient, but a candidate for life or death aneurysm repair.) The nurse readying to shave me explained that the vein harvested for the bypasses could come from anywhere – leg or arm. And that sometimes urgent access to the heart via an artery from the groin was necessary. That was why I was to get the whole-of-body shave – scrotum inclusive.

It soon became apparent that as 'a hairy man' the task was too much for the one nurse who became asthmatically wheezy and so she called a female colleague to come to assist her. By about 8.45pm, the job was done. Zandra and Anthea visited to say 'goodnight'. My body was now ready for vein harvesting as part of bypass surgery. I felt as if I had undergone some kind of pagan ritual in preparation for human sacrifice.

Coronory Artery Bypass

Harvesting a vein to create a bypass of a blocked coronary artery is a technique first performed in 1967 by Rene Favaloro, an Argentine surgeon, at the Cleveland Clinic in the USA. These days, Coronary Artery Bypass (CAB) surgery is such a common procedure nearly everyone in Australia will have a relative or friend who's experienced it. It was in the early 1960s that less successful forms of the procedure began. With CAB the chest is opened to reveal the heart by sawing apart the sternum (breast bone), which at the end of the operation is securely stapled together again. The invention of the modern heart-lung machine – to both oxygenate, and also to eliminate carbon dioxide from, the patient's blood – has allowed the heart to be stopped for the bypasses to be grafted in. Surprisingly, Maximilian von Frey at the University of Leipzig constructed a crude version of this type of machine as early as 1885. Though it was not until the 1960s – after a decade or so of experimentation on dogs and some early failures with humans – that the modern machine was invented and used with repeated success. This simple summary belies the sophisticated science and technology that evolved to make CAB so successful that these days, even after this most invasive surgery, a patient with no complications can expect to leave hospital about five days after the operation.

It was not male prudishness or some form of sexism that made the shaving so traumatic. Though there was probably an element of both in my reaction. As will be obvious to amateur psychologists through my continual mention of that very private male part, the scrotum. Weeks later, I realised I was distressed about my transformed body image – the hairy man turned into the smooth-skinned man. But the major distress was 'loss of control trauma'. The passivity of becoming an object at the hands of others, the perennial 'being a patient' anxiety. It was only in retrospect that the depth of this trauma, its metaphysics – the objectification of the self – became apparent to me. I used to think being in control or losing control was mostly a male psychological issue. But in our modern secular-consumer individualistic culture, it is clearly gender-inclusive.

There is nothing like submitting to surgery when it comes to loss of control!

PEACEFUL SLEEP AGAIN

Three weeks previously, on the night of my heart attack - in spite of that overwhelming, foreboding sense of impending doom - through the Jesus Prayer, I managed to get to sleep. Getting to sleep when you have been told that your heart could burst at any moment. And when next morning, if you survive the night, you are to undergo surgery with a predicted 50-50 chance of survival, is a much bigger challenge. I was given a sleeping pill. But I do not think for one moment that it was a chemical induced peacefulness that engulfed my consciousness and allowed me to sleep. Rather it was a spiritual peace. Not the Jesus Prayer this time; rather, it came from deep meditation on a Biblical text.

As priest and bishop, I have conducted a very large number of funerals in my time. So as I lay immobile in bed that night, contemplating the 50-50 predicted chance, it is not surprising that the Anglican funeral service came to mind. (I had primed my family during the afternoon with suggestions of what, in the event of my death, I would like to happen at my funeral.) To begin a service of burial or cremation, the *Australian Anglican Prayer Book* (AAPB) gives the following directive to the clergy officiant:

When the body is brought to the cemetery, or to the crematorium, the minister meets it at the entrance. He says one or more of the following sentences, as he goes before the body towards the grave or into the chapel...'

It was the first of these listed Biblical sentences that became my earworm on surgery eve. Translated from the original Greek, written two thousand years previously by Paul the Apostle as part of a letter to the fledgling Christian community in imperial Rome, it says:

If we live, we live to the Lord, and if we die, we die to the Lord; so then, whether we live or whether we die, we are the Lord's.

Over and over and over, the rhythmic prose of this text echoed – body, mind, psyche and spirit – in the depths of my being. A mantra of assurance!

I will say more about how this text affected me – to the depths – when we get to the recovery period of my story. Enough to say here that the meaning of these words – and please forgive my word-twisting as it's the only way I can get near to expressing what I knew and felt – became meaning in itself, pure and simple meaning, beyond words. Or to put it another way, still straining for words I cannot find, the meaning became me and I became the meaning. In this 'safe way-of-being', I had no fear of death or of the manner by which death might come. I slept soundly. Early next morning, still in this same 'safe way-of-being', I greeted Zandra and Anthea, hugged goodbye, and was wheeled on a trolley to the operating theatre.

ICU

Next for me came waking to semi-conscious awareness. Then spending four or five days in the Intensive Care Unit (ICU) of Westmead Hospital. Some staff clearly assumed that I was unconscious, possibly because I was attached to an artificial respirator. To my anguish, they joked about the recent death of a doctor, whom they clearly disliked intensely. He had the same surname, 'Wilson', as mine. Death and Wilson caused much amusement, but certainly not to me in my circumstance. Afterwards, I thought this may have been a nasty hallucination or dream. But at home, weeks later, I found the appropriate death notice on the Internet.

As theological students and trainee priests learning the practice of pastoral-care, we had been firmly warned always to assume that a seemingly unconscious person might actually be aware of what was happening around them. An important principle when as a priest or pastor one is so often called to a deathbed for prayers and anointing (sometimes called the 'last rites'). It was not unusual in my experience for a dying, seemingly totally 'unconscious' patient, to utter 'amen' at the conclusion of a prayer I'd just said over them. It is amazing that ICU nurses in a major hospital seem not to have been taught this wisdom.

Another nurse had the task of applying a suction tube to remove excess fluid from my mouth. She constantly poked it hard into my soft palette, carelessly causing pain. Unable to speak in protest – with deflated lungs and hooked up to all manner of tubes and wires – I dreaded her working shifts. I made murderous mental plans for her future. But I imagine that she, too, thought I was unconscious and could not feel anything.

A wonderful memory of ICU is the sheer physical joy of being taken off the respirator to breathe on my own again. 'Breathe, Bruce, breathe', in my groggy state I heard a nurse commanding over and over. 'Breathe, Bruce, breathe.' And I did.

It was exhilarating. Producing that same feeling of life-infusion that one got as a child after swimming underwater for too long and coming up for air.

I did not leave hospital after the usual few days sojourn typical of the usual CAB patients, but after a few weeks. A delay caused not by post-surgery complications – of which thankfully there were none – but because aneurysm and aneurysm repair were more serious and complex conditions than CAB itself. As young Dr Bill Lyons had explained, my heart could have burst at any moment as it was held together only by blood clots and the heart sac. But my impatience to leave hospital became more and more acute. I became inwardly resentful as wave after wave of CAB patients in my ward went home. From my ambulance trip down the mountains to open heart surgery itself, everything happened so quickly that no one had explained to me the magnitude of my operation. Or the level of recovery involved. As I say in **Kickstart,** it was only…

> Later I learnt that a 'pseudo' was in fact worse than a 'real' aneurysm. The latter is a ballooning and thinning of tissue that has not formed into a hole or tear. I also learnt that the pseudo-aneurysm did actually burst in the hands of my surgeon but fortunately I was then connected up to the bypass machine. The surgeon cleared the blood clots and then sewed a Gore-Tex patch over the hole.
>
> By the time I heard about the bursting and the patch, I was on the road to recovery but I burst into tears when the pictures of those things formed in my

mind. That's something else I've learnt through all my heart troubles – 'forget that blokey idea of a stiff upper lip, when upset have a good cry, it does you heaps of good physically as well as emotionally and spiritually'.

Gore-Tex, I knew, was what some wind-cheater jackets you can buy in Kathmandu shops are made of. For some reason it upset me very much to think of my poor little heart pumping away the lifeblood inside me all patched-up with stuff people wear on the snowfields. Months later, I felt much better, even a little superior, when my surgeon told me that Gore-Tex was first invented for surgery and only later made useful for skiers and bushwalkers.

Transferred to the cardiac recovery ward, hooked up to Wi-Fi monitors transmitting every heartbeat to the Nurses' Station, I was given a Teddy Bear. At least it was called a 'Teddy Bear'. In actual fact, it was a small pillow that you were meant to clutch to your breast. Post-operative pain after open heart surgery is concentrated in the area of the wire-stapled sternum. One's Teddy Bear is not only intended to be a physical comfort and an emotional solace – as are 'real' Teddy Bears for us as children – but also to assist with minimising pain-causing chest movement. Thanks to sedatives, almost the only time post-operative pain became acutely uncomfortable was when – daily – the physiotherapist visited, commanding 'cough' in order to ensure one's lungs were clear and pneumonia was not developing. Laughter was nearly as painful as coughing. Causing me to hold tight to Teddy, and to smile only, in order to repress convulsions at the witty jokes cracked constantly by the nursing staff.

For the first ten days or so in the cardiac recovery ward, I experienced what I can only describe as 'floating on the Sea of Death'. Whenever I closed my eyes – and feeling so desperately ill that was much of the time – I felt myself buoyed up by a vast, heaving, completely deep-grey sea under a near, featureless but lighter grey sky. There was no horizon. No other world. Nothing except me and the grey sea and sky. Looking back, I interpret this experience as the mental visualisation of being constantly on the edge of actual death.

The hallucinatory sea was not attractive but not threatening either. It buoyed me up and carried me on the rhythms of its swells. Unafraid, I was content to float along wherever it carried me. There was no sense that I might drown. Or sink in it to oblivion. Only later did I connect – as a possible source of the imagery for this inner hallucinatory experience – the impossible feat two decades previously of trying to sink not float in Israel's Dead (or Salt) Sea.

STRANGE CONVERSATIONS

During this time, I experienced 'hallucinatory' conversations with a close friend and sometime mentor, Owen Dowling. A few months previously, Owen had been diagnosed with advanced throat cancer. He had been Canberra's Anglican bishop, famous nationwide for his advocacy of women as priests. By this time, Owen had returned to Canberra after a sojourn as vicar of a

Tasmanian parish. That appointment followed from damaging publicity arising from homosexual entrapment by a policeman at a park in a Victorian country town. Living with his pending death, Owen was creating beautiful, reflective poems that he emailed to friends. As I lay 'floating on the Sea of Death', our conversation included discussion of who should die first – me or him?

Owen died on May 7, 2008. Ten days after my heart surgery. More than a month later, on June 13, 2008 I wrote to his wife:

> Dear Gloria,
>
> Today, with my apology, is the first day I have had the psychic and physical strength to send this email to convey my love and prayers to you and to explain that I was unable to attend Owen's funeral because I myself was in hospital with the expectation, continuous over a three-week period, that I could die at any moment. Zandra even withheld news of Owen's passing from me knowing how upset I would be and the possible consequences.
>
> In some of my delirious states I found myself talking to Owen, including discussing which of us would die first - he being very surprised that I was so close to him in this.
>
> When I discovered that I was still alive and that Owen had died I wept and wept, and wept again when I realised that I could not even honour him and you by attending his funeral.

> *You and Owen have been in my prayers all through Owen's illnesses, you both remain deep in those prayers.*
>
> *Blessings and Love,*
> *Bruce*

PRAYER PROBLEMS

Night after night during this time, and several times during some days as well, nursing staff would rush to my bedside once again asking 'Are you all right, Mr Wilson?' My answer, resentfully when I was still more asleep than awake, was always a socially polite 'Yes, I'm fine, thanks'. Gradually, I ceased feeling 'fine'. Disquieted by the realisation that the staff were responding to Wi-Fi heart monitors registering dangerous, possibly deadly, arrhythmias at the nurses' station.

This was a period when consciously and intentionally I wanted to pray.

At first, I was troubled by what to pray. You may think that was easy – 'pray for healing, pray to get better, pray that God will give wisdom to those treating you'. My inner audience chimed in mockingly -'Fancy a bishop not knowing how to pray!' But what if I was meant to die not live? What do you pray then? And what the bloody-hell does being a bishop have to do with it? A bishop is called to humble service not special privilege! And why should God pay particular attention to the prayers of an old man like me. An affluent cosseted, privileged 'First-Worlder'. When in

Third World countries God 'permits', if that is the correct word, thousands of children and babies to die from cheaply treatable diseases? Floating on the Sea of Death, these were prayer-paralysing questions for me.

A BIGGER BIT ABOUT GOD

The question of God as such was not an issue. After a lengthy flirtation, I rejected atheism in my early twenties. It failed to fit the facts of my human moral and spiritual experience. Actual experience not theory.

We live in two worlds. Uniquely so, until and unless we discover there are extra- terrestrials who share our mysterious, reflective self-conscious way of being alive. Just like all other creatures, we live a material, animal life. Like most of them, we breathe the air, digest our food, sexually procreate, sneeze and defecate. But unlike them, we are transcendental creatures. We are of the earth earthy, just like rabbits or elephants. But we are of the transcendent transcendentally, like nothing else. We die like every other creature, but we alone imagine and anticipate our death.

The second creation story of Adam and Eve in the ancient Hebrew Bible (Old Testament) explores our double nature. It contains a witty play on words. The Hebrew word *adam* means 'man' and the Hebrew *adamah* means 'earth'. God forms man(kind) from the dust of the ground – Adam is of the earth, earthy - but then God infuses Adam with the Divine breath itself – so the human becomes transcendent, transcendentally; earthy and divine.

Our double nature is a regular theme in literature. Shakespeare explores it, for example, via a melancholy Hamlet who both marvels and bemoans thus:

> What a piece of work is man, how noble in reason, how infinite in faculty, In form and moving how express and admirable, In action how like an Angel, In apprehension how like a god, The beauty of the world, The paragon of animals. And yet to me, what is this quintessence of dust? Man delights not me; no, nor Woman neither.

In 1975, I left my position as Anglican chaplain to the University of NSW to take a up an appointment as Rector (parish pastor/priest) at Paddington in inner city Sydney. While tidying up the Rectory front garden just after moving in, I was greeted by a neighbour who bade me welcome, explained he was a professor at a nearby university and that he was an atheist. I asked him what God/s he didn't believe in. His description/definition was little more sophisticated than Sigmund Freud's Sky Father. And by that description, I was probably a more radical atheist than he was.

As I understand it, the meaning of the English word G-O-D (God) contains direct experience of the Transcendental. Manifest in a number of intrinsic dimensions of our actual experience in the Lifeworld, briefly summarised here.

Reason is the Transcendent Light by which we find our way in the world and come to understand how things work. Only Reason can justify Reason. Which is the same as saying its reality is irreducible, it **just *is*** – and it works! Thanks to the careful application of Reason we have such wonders as modern medicine and such honourable disciplines as philosophy, theology and science.

Conscience, too, is a direct irreducible experience. The Transcendent Voice of right and wrong, good and evil. Even allowing for obvious social and historical variations, the knowledge of right and wrong, of good and evil **just is**. At the ultimate, this distinction cannot be explained by anything else either. We just know in our heart of hearts, and mind of minds, what is right and what is wrong. A voice that judges us all.

Aesthetics – the experiences of Beauty – music perhaps most of all, a symphony, a sunset, a face, a painting, a landscape – sublime beyond words to express. Emotion and meaning that also **just is.**

Love – a grab-bag word, but in its highest forms, say *eros* and *agape*, a value even most atheists treat as transcendental, an indefinable **just is.**

Self-Consciousness - not just knowing but also knowing that we know – the foundation of all our **just is**, transcendental experiences. God's breath in us, our own image of God.

There is absolutely nothing new in all this. For millennia these experiences have been called our natural knowledge of God.

All the deepest thinking about God has always said that God **just is**. Or more technically, that God is ***ens a se*** (of his/her own being). God **just is.**

The perennial schoolboy question 'Who made God?' derives from a shallow and silly picture of what the word 'God' means.

It already assumes that 'God' is some sort of a **thing** among all other things. That is a very shrivelled idea of God. God is not just some sort of being among beings – say like a galaxy, a fish or a microbe – God is Being behind beings. 'God' means the Transcendental One, the Most High, the Creator and Sustainer of the whole Lifeworld. The One who is in and through all things. The One who is beyond and above all things. Immanent and transcendent!

Classical atheists, such as Karl Marx, Sigmund Freud and Bertrand Russell, say we make God in our own image. The theist says that we are made in God's image. It might seem an odd way to put it, but the theist says that we are tiny transcendentals. Spiritually, microscopic images of God.

Science And Religion In 398 A.d. – Augustine

Amazing how little has changed - Augustine accused some of the scientists of his day of ignoring consciousness, thus becoming anthropocentric – human not God centred. They use reason, he complained, in order to understand the Lifeworld but they don't acknowledge that by trusting reason they are invoking a reality more deeply rooted and structured than themselves. Instead of recognising with awe that they are uncovering the mind of God, they praise themselves. Addressing God, he says:

You come close only to men who are humble at heart. The proud cannot find you, even though by dint of study they have skill to number the stars and grains of sand, to measure the tracts of constellations and trace the paths of planets...

The reason and understanding by which they investigate these things are gifts they have from you. By means of them they have discovered much and foretold eclipses of the sun and moon many years before they happened.

They calculated the day and the hour of the eclipse, and whether it would be total or partial, and their reckonings were found correct because it all happened as they had predicted…

These powers are a source of wonder and astonishment to men who do not know the secrets. But the astronomers are flattered and claim the credit for themselves. They lapse into pride without respect for you, my God… This is because they ignore you and do not inquire how they come to posses the intelligence to make these researches.

PRAYER RESUMED

One way or another, I imagine nearly everyone facing critical illness and possible death asks the big questions about God again. As I said, my prayer issue was not about God as such. About, rather, what God is like and how we relate to God. About how God relates to us.

God, understood as a remote TRANSCENDENTAL ULTIMATE REALITY – though directly and universally experienced through Reason and Conscience – is not much help or comfort in any circumstance. Let alone in the face of death and dying. In these situations, God questions are **gut** questions, not **mind** questions.

My needs were desperate. Though reduced to the state of a quivering sick animal, I still wanted to pray intelligently not stupidly. Childlike yes! Childishly no! To reach out to the real God, not a god made in my own image. To be a dependent adult. Not a dependent child.

Though for me the question of God as such is not an issue – the question of God's relationship to me, to nature, to the Lifeworld itself, is a big, live and confusing issue. Especially when it comes to prayers that ask God to do things. Petitionary prayers, such as 'Please heal me', 'Save me from death'.

I know lots of people who hit God daily with shopping lists of such requests. Petitionary prayers asking for everything from good health and weather – 'rain please' or 'sunny please' – to peace in the Middle East or the cure of a neighbour from cancer. To me, these seem pretty crazy, irrational ideas about how God relates to us. Even crazier when the lists include such things as work promotions, or what suburb to live in, or what make of car to buy ('Will that be with metallic paint, madam?'). I even know one guy who requests God to show him which bus to catch to town. Sometimes leaving him waiting at the bus stop for hours until 'God' gives the nod.

It is easy to criticise and make fun of many petitionary prayers. Yet even the most irrational of them indicates something deep about the precariousness and potential meaninglessness of our lives. About our contingency. About the afflictions and evils that beset us and our Lifeworld.

'Petitionary Prayer' is only one form of prayer but it poses the most problems to our modern, scientifically conditioned minds. It's a question of ***if, when, and how*** God intervenes in the normal observed patterns and regularities of the 'material' realm of the Lifeworld. Experience demonstrates that God does not normally interfere. If God did, we would be living in a random, unpredictable and thus extremely unsettling world.

Most prayer is simply relating to God in various ways – by meditating, keeping silence, practising solitude or simply chatting with God as one might with a friend.

My advice to people who are troubled about how or what to pray is usually – *'Forget God, just find a quiet place that is physically comfortable, but not too comfortable, be silent, then after a while speak to the deepest part of your own self* **with complete truthfulness.**' That last phrase is critical!

Prayer is being open to the Divine Presence. Discovering God within and being discovered there. Much more about listening than speaking. It is certainly not first and foremost about a 'Santa Claus' style gift-list. Not even for such a worthy Christmas present as heart health.

If we only try to pray when we are in deep trouble – forgive the semantics – we will find it very hard to pray **when we are** in deep trouble. We will feel spiritually embarrassed. Like a silly child asking for Divine magic tricks. And in our very own eyes, we will make God look like Sigmund Freud's Sky Father. The phantom projection of an insecure infant's imagination. I have laboured hard and long in spiritual guidance with such people. For example, newly diagnosed cancer patients, helping them to accept that God will graciously hear them regardless of their long neglect.

As a fact, I *was* in deep trouble – floating on the Sea of Death – feeling desperately ill. It was Petitionary Prayer time

– but what form of petition? Emotionally I was screaming out 'God help me'. I wanted it to be more than that, but what?

Nearly four decades earlier in my first book - **The Human Journey:** *Christianity and Modern Consciousness* – I told a story about how I prayed when facing a similar dilemma. Back then, my anxiety was not about my health but about my father's. The issue was throat cancer and this is the prayer I prayed:

> *Lord, you already know that my father has a tumour and you already know that I don't want him to die. I know that someday he will die and that I will have to cope without his friendship, but does it have to be so soon? You know his fears and that he feels he still has lots of things to live for here. Let him know that he is in your hands whatever happens. If he has to die soon, let us both feel your love even if we cannot presently understand your design. Amen.*

Dad died 18 years later, but from a heart attack not cancer. By then, he had quietly and privately let go of his atheism.

To me now, that prayer is too contrived, cold, bloodless, calculated and embarrassing. Yet in a shallow way, floating on the Sea of Death, it mirrored the gist of the short prayers I prayed about myself. Unlike the prayer for my father's healing, these prayers had no formal structure or careful wording. Floating on the Sea of Death hardly evokes reflective, prudent creations. These prayers were short emotional outbursts. There was, though, a similar attempt amidst emotional mayhem to address the Creator of the Lifeworld intelligently as well as desperately.

Their content can be summed up as 'God, hold me', 'Lord, comfort me', 'Strengthen me', 'God, heal me'. 'Heal me to this life'. 'Heal me through death'. 'Give me the grace just to be, in You'.

(Some of my pastoral ministry over many decades has involved assisting the dying to experience the healing **through** death. Our post-Christian culture – enthralled by the success of modern medicine to heal us **from** death, or at least to postpone it - has lost the knowledge of the healing **through** death. This, sadly, is even true of most clergy, who see their ministry more as teachers and leaders than healers. Significantly, the **Cure of Souls** is the traditional phrase used by my Church to describe the ministry of a priest or pastor.)

A BLOCK OF CONCRETE

'Whew! Whammy! These heart problems come at you from nowhere, at least that's how it feels!' This is what I wrote in **Kickstart** to describe the physical effects of my heart attack, open-heart surgery and what followed. I had no idea that I was about to be assailed by a spiritual *'Whew! Whammy!'* too.

Floating on the Sea of Death in the Cardiac Recovery Ward, as I tried to pray, I encountered a previously unimaginable obstacle. The only picture of God that formed in my head was of an infinite, benign but indifferent, block of concrete.

How do you pray to a block of concrete? Where did that image come from? How could I, a traditionally orthodox mainstream Christian, have such a bizarre image of God? Wasn't this heretical? Was it idolatrous? Was it atheistic? Isn't God personal? Sure personal! But personal beyond our imagination - an infinite personal. How can you picture an infinite personal? Will a picture of a block of concrete do it? Surely not!

These questions later became huge. As my patched-up heart and stapled- together sternum were mending, I grappled with them as part of the spiritual mending of my dismembered psycho-spiritual self. But just as I did not experience the Sea of Death as hostile, neither did I find the infinite Block of Concrete disturbing or threatening. Both images, and they were dream-like real – not just mental thoughts or consciously imaginative constructs – left me feeling quite peaceful. That amazed me. And down the track, troubled me.

IMPLANTED ANGEL

The heart arrhythmias – the dangers of which I was now fully aware – did not go away. This, in spite of taking the maximum safe level of Beta-Blocker drugs meant to control them. Lloyd Davis, my default cardiologist, specialises in heart rhythms. He decided I needed another (invasive) procedure to see if my heart was likely to go into Ventricular Fibrillation - VF. Another Whew! Whammy!

In simple terms, VF means that instead of the heart beating rhythmically at a normal 70 or 80 beats a minute, the lower chambers – the ventricles – just wildly quiver or flutter (fibrillate). VF ruins the heart's blood-pumping action. Without intervention, death follows in minutes. VF is the major cause of sudden death among heart attack victims, including horses.

An Unwelcome Visitor

Staged annually in November, the Melbourne Cup – Australia's premier horse race – is a major event on the international racing calendar. At the 2014 race, a Japanese horse named *Admire Rakti* was the much-fancied favourite to win the $3.6 million first place prize-money. The day after the running of the cup, Melbourne's *Herald Sun* newspaper reported this tragedy:

> The Japanese galloper started favourite in Tuesday's 3200m Melbourne Cup but was pulled out of the race with 500m to go. He later collapsed and died in his stall.
>
> Racing Victoria's Dr Brian Stewart said an autopsy revealed Admire Rakti died of ventricular fibrillation – an abnormal, irregular heart rhythm with uncoordinated electrical activity and contractions. Because the ventricles do not contract, blood does not circulate.

The race was won by a German horse, *Protectionist*, with *Admire Rakti* officially last.

The invasive procedure performed to test if my heart was vulnerable to ventricular fibrillation is called an Intracardiac Electrophysiology Study – EPS for short. Still floating on the Sea of Death, unable without assistance to get out of bed to sit in a hospital soft chair, you can imagine how I felt about another operation! It took two weeks of gentle persuasion before I took the leap to saying 'yes'. And then mostly because Dr Davis would not agree to officiously discharge me from hospital unless I had an EPS.

An EPS puts the heart's electrical 'wiring' to the test. Going through the groin, a catheter is fed up into the heart, placing electrodes along the heart's conductive system to measure its electrical activity. The electrodes can detect abnormal beats and are used to test if fibrillation can be induced or not. Unfortunately, 'not' didn't apply to me – my heart's electrics were readily subject to deadly ventricular fibrillation. I don't know if this is scientifically accurate, but my guess was that the Gore-Tex patch interfered with the normal electrical activity of my heart. As with most medical and surgical procedures, solving one problem often creates another. Side effects they are usually called. Though 'broadside' effects would frequently be more accurate.

After the EPS, Dr Davis said that to avoid the likely possibility of sudden death, I would need an ICD – an Implantable Cardioverter-Defibrillator. Thanks to a spate of media coverage, including stories about the installation of portable defibrillators in train stations, convention centres, sports clubhouses and other public venues, the defibrillator is a better-known device now than it was back in mid 2008.

Implantable Cardioverter Defibrillator

To my amazement, I discovered doing research that, in principle at least, defibrillators were first 'invented' in 1899 when Jean-Louis Prevost and Frederic Batelli of the University of Geneva demonstrated that small electrical shocks could induce ventricular fibrillation in dogs. And that a larger shock could reverse the condition. The first successful use on a human did not occur until 1947. Until the early 1950s, human heart defibrillation was only possible when the chest cavity was surgically opened. The first modern ICD – with its sophisticated computer technology and algorithms – was implanted in February 1980 at John Hopkins University in the USA. Today, these devices can even, if needed, be implanted in small babies shortly after birth.

In the chapter I contributed to John England's explain-things-simply book **Kickstart**, I christened the defibrillator 'My Guardian Angel'. Having told the story of the EPS procedure, I went on:

> My Guardian Angel has batteries and she was surgically fitted several days later just under the skin below my left shoulder blade. Technically, she's called a defibrillator, a word that took me weeks to pronounce and spell correctly. Sometimes it's easier, though, to tell people I have a pacemaker. These devices that electrically regulate slow beating hearts have been around longer, so are better known, and what they do is easier to understand.
>
> When I learnt that my heart was prone to deadly fibrillation, I, and my whole family, were scared stiff about my leaving the safety of hospital. At least in hospital if my heart fibrillated or stopped beating it could be corrected or re-started by one of those big two-handled electric-pad defibrillators that you see doctors jolting heart attack patients back to life with in films and on TV. Some people call them Packer-Whackers, named after the media mogul Kerry Packer who donated smaller version defibrillators for use in every NSW ambulance after his own life was saved by one.

Every day could be a bit of a nervous nightmare for me and my family without my Guardian Angel. She monitors every single beat of my heart — that's about a hundred thousand beats a day — week in week out, month in month out, making sure my ticker's ticking properly.

If my Guardian Angel detects any deadly fibrillations, she first sends some electrical pulses down through the lead that goes via a vein into my heart to slow things down. If that doesn't do the trick, then she'll give the heart a good electrical jolt, causing it to restart in a regular, paced rhythm.

Every three or six months, I have to go for interrogation. I love to say to my acquaintances, 'Got to get interrogated tomorrow'. Naturally, they wonder what dreadful thing I must have done that means I have to face up to ASIO or the Federal Police; and I enjoy letting them wonder.

Actually, it means the manufacturers wirelessly hook my defibrillator up to their computer, print a read out of any therapy episodes she's performed and make any necessary fine tunings. The fun part is when the test temporarily speeds up my heart rate at the press of a computer button.

Two days after implantation of the defibrillator, Dr Lloyd Davis agreed that I could leave hospital and go home. It was Friday May 16, 2008. This marked the start of an intense few months of psychological, spiritual and metaphysical experiences. As I said,

I discovered that patching up the heart had dismembered my spirit, so now a double healing was needed – a new patching.

In readiness for the drive home, Zandra and Anthea packed up their belongings and vacated the apartment they'd rented adjacent to the hospital. Their close presence provided me with wonderful support during the post-operative stages of my hospital stay.

This was by tragic contrast to a rural indigenous man recovering from bypass surgery in a bed next to mine. He did not have a single visitor. In my condition, I could pray for him, converse a little, but that was about all. Inwardly, I moaned to God – in whose eyes we two old blokes were equal – about the injustice of social inequality with its delivery of privilege and non-privilege. All my adult life, I had joined hands with movements seeking to eliminate this injustice. At one time, for example, chairing the Native Title Task Force of the National Council of Churches. But here in a hospital ward was a reminder of the ongoing disparity between indigenous and non-indigenous. His mob – by contrast with my non-indigenous mob – did not have the money to rent a Sydney apartment!

Thanking all the wonderful hospital staff for their care and skills, being wished umpteen 'good lucks' in return, we headed for the car park. My body weight had dropped almost twenty kilograms. I needed support to walk. The thought of living in the new, half-moved-into Leura house was alienating and psychically abominable. I needed familiarity, a warm recovery nest. So the Mt Victoria retreat was taken off the market and there we settled for the coming winter months.

A measure of how ill I still felt was an inability to have my beloved Henry around me. He would want the usual play. And to sit for hours on my lap. A close friend, the Rev. Aniko Koro, whom I had ordained when bishop of Bathurst Diocese, cared for him while I was in hospital. She happily agreed to keep him until I was ready to have him home. When her work permitted, Aniko also shared with Zandra the task of accompanying me on my twice a day, recovery walks. It was unsafe to walk alone. They started as five-minute indoor walks, morning and afternoon. Then ten minutes outdoors, then fifteen. After a couple of months, they morphed into one forty-five minute outdoor walk each day. I attribute my continuing survival as much to these daily walks as to my medications or my defibrillator. They are physical and psychical saviours.

By a letter to both of us, Lloyd Davis handed me over to John England for heart specialist care, alleviating the long drives to Westmead Hospital in Sydney. As mentioned earlier, I see John as an eccentric saint. He has a beautiful, caring manner with all his patients and is dedicated to his profession as a vocation above any material rewards. He only bills his patients the government paid Medicare rebate. He is a spiritual person. When I attend a consultation, he always has a back-copy of the excellent English Catholic magazine, **The Tablet,** to pass on to me. He is subject to up-days and down-days, the former characterised by running extremely late with appointments as he enjoys chats with his multifarious patients. Noting the crush in the waiting room on such days, I learn to steer him away from theological discussion onto my heart health.

Along with all members of his profession, John needs to watch his use of words. Medical terminology is always rather abstruse to patients. Sometimes it is totally confusing or frightening. At my first consultation, he informed me that I had 'Congestive Heart Failure' and gave me a photocopy of an article about making an advanced health care directive. Zandra and I left that consultation with the impression that I probably had just weeks or, at best, months to live. I made an immediate appointment to see Andrew Masterton, my GP. Specifically to ask him how long he thought I had left and whether we should put the Leura house on the market. He was amused, and spoke of patients with Congestive Heart Failure he'd been managing for years. (Six months later, I had recovered sufficiently to move into the Leura house.)

It's the word 'failure' that's the trouble. It connotes something ominously immediate and abrupt. John England did not invent the terminology; it is widely used in cardiology. The four stages of the New York Congestive Heart Failure Classification system are a major diagnostic tool. But 'Congestive Heart Disease', would be a better term – descriptively accurate but not so threatening to patients.

The early months of recovery were quite difficult. Within weeks, I was back in hospital emergency – this time at the small Blue Mountains District Hospital – with fluid on my lungs (Congestive Heart Failure indeed!). Constantly overcome with fatigue, I slept half the day and all the night. Not much of a crier in the past, I could hardly have a conversation now without at some point sobbing tearfully. Worst of all was the extreme nausea, a side-effect of the heart strengthening drug digitalis. Amazingly, this drug, sourced from the foxglove plant and first described by William Withering in 1785, still remains a top-line treatment for 'powering-up' the contractions of weak hearts like mine.

I did not know what lay ahead. I was just grateful to be home. I did know that in so many ways – physically, psychologically, metaphysically and spiritually – I was not the same person and never would be again. Critical illness and a visit to death's door are life-changers. This was not the end of a story, only of a chapter.

*Lifeworld

'Lifeworld' is about our spectacles, not what we look at but what we look through. 'Seeing the world through rose coloured glasses' is a popular way of saying that someone is being unrealistically optimistic. We only realise that we *always* see things through spectacles when someone asks 'Why do you think that?' or 'Why do you do that?' - and realise how feeble is an answer 'Well, that's just how things are'. My critique of what's happening today is that people seem to be wearing blinkers with their spectacles. And are unaware of either!

Given authority to dictate a language change, I would replace the word 'Universe' with 'Lifeworld'. This would release our minds from the rut of an idea that the 'Universe' (in current popular usage) is only something external to us. We might then begin to recognise again that the totality of our human experience, the Lifeworld, always has these three ingredients to it:

* Consciousness (shared with all the animal kingdom and maybe all the biosphere)

* That of which we are conscious (currently and wrongly thought of as 'the universe')

* Self-Consciousness (in degree uniquely human).

'Lifeworld' is everything we experience. All phenomena. From dreams to galaxies – the whole show, all that there is. It derives from a school of philosophy known as Phenomenology but we don't need to go into that.

'Universe' is not a good enough word anymore because it no longer means 'the whole show' -everything. Instead, it refers to a restricted range of phenomena. Today, 'universe' usually means the space-time physical phenomena – from the sub-atomic to the cosmological. This 'universe' includes the totally false assumption that it encompasses all that there is. Consciousness, self-consciousness, good, evil, love and beauty are not included.

To exclude consciousness, for example, is to eliminate the knower from the known. An absurdity. A simple way of putting this is to say, there are no sights 'out there' apart from eyes, no smells apart from noses, no sounds apart from ears, no worldviews apart from minds. What is 'out there' – if 'out there' has any meaning at all except for 'perceptions of experiences that human beings agree they share in common' - always involves consciousness.

Alfred North Whitehead, mathematician and philosopher of science, is one of the few voices outspokenly and devastatingly critical of the elimination of consciousness from the so-called scientific worldview. He says that science continually commits an error that he calls 'The

Fallacy of Misplaced Concreteness'. He means, first, the separation of an 'out there' world from the human consciousness that perceives it. Then, second, the construction of scientific models of that separated world which are misleadingly treated as if they are the real world. Metaphysically equivalent to a psychotic creating castles-in-the-air and then moving in.

Whitehead says that the only real world (his 'prehensive' world) is the world in which consciousness and that-of-which-we-are-conscious are inextricably commingled. He says that from the seventeenth century on, the Western World has been increasingly deceived into believing that a purely Physicalist/Materialist abstraction is the real world. It has benefited the West materially and technologically but at great spiritual cost.

PART 2

A Welcome Visitor

At the start I said:

> *How we respond to major afflictions in our lives is either our making or our breaking. My purpose in telling the following story is not to focus morbidly or self-indulgently on life-threatening illness and the hazards and benefits of modern medical practice. Others have suffered much worse and more complicated afflictions than mine. But rather to explore the profound existential, spiritual, ethical and metaphysical transformations that brushes with mortality engender. With the prospect that my story may give others insight, courage and hope. It is a story about finding deeper meaning.*

So far, the story has been a story of physical patch-ups: of hospitals, doctors, nurses, surgical operations, investigative procedures, medical errors and a prosthetic implant. It was a wonderful relief to be out of hospital – home. But it will take well over a year before my body 'recovers' from all the assaults on it. ***Recover*** means becoming the best it can ever be. With its patched-up disabilities, my body is never going to be the same again.

As my body healed, I knew that in profound ways my mind and spirit, too, would never be the same again. Amazingly, I was to become more deeply rooted and grounded existentially, spiritually, ethically and metaphysically than ever before. Via all the twists and turns, ups and downs, eventually I found myself able to say to myself – 'Bless you heart attack for being in my life'.

Maybe it's my personal history, my genes - or maybe I am just a bit wacky! But I don't get it when I see people who've been afflicted by serious illness, who've hovered over death's abyss, appear to resume their lives as if nothing had happened.

I try to work out how this can be. To me it seems like watching a fearful caterpillar. Forced without choice from its cocoon into a world of new – and yes challenging – unknown horizon, it tries to spin mangled and broken threads back into the old, familiar – seemingly secure - cocoon. Impossible, of course. Denial of reality.

Maybe this is because our secular-consumer, materialist society has cruelled our ability to take on the challenge of psychic and spiritual adventures: reducing our exploratory instincts to the physical. We trek high mountains, scuba dive deep oceans, aspire to visit outer space. But we ignore or evade the sheers, cliffs, hills, plains, oceans and deserts of inner-space - of mind, psyche and spirit. Perhaps the latter are too challenging? We have a fear of psycho-spiritual flying?

SHAVED OF IDENTITY

I am no diarist or journal keeper but, from my teenage years on, whenever I am overwhelmed by my feelings, especially by negative feelings – anger, confusion, lust, hate, anxiety, depression, revenge etc. – I externalise them on paper. I just let my feelings pour out randomly in any words that come. An uncontrolled, reflective, stream of consciousness. They are usually reflections on past events that impinge on present experience. It is my way of acquiring some sort of 'handle' on myself. Getting it out onto the page helps me to 'get myself together'. To make sense of what is happening. Discover some sort of order out of chaos.

Back in the security of home, I began to experience traumatic feelings of confusion about my new identity. I've added the title, but otherwise here exactly is part of what I wrote shortly after getting out of hospital:

Who Am I? The Shaving.
Like the Biblical patriarch Jacob's brother Esau, I am a hairy man. Open heart surgery plus stripped me of my identity. I almost wrote my 'old' identity but that's not how it was. It stripped me of my identity, stripped me of me.
It began about 8.30 pm on the night of April 25 (Anzac Day evening, St Mark's Day), five hours earlier the surgeon had said, 'unless you have this operation you will be dead in a couple of days'. By dead, he meant nothing metaphysical, psychological or spiritual. No one told me though 'if you have this operation and live, you – the you that you know is you – will be dead when it is all over.'

It began with the shaving, as I said, about 8.30 pm. The shaver itself looked a bit like an oversized safety razor and was operated by the same handle pulling motion, except it was battery operated. The operator was a kindly nurse, overweight and with a slight asthmatic wheeze, in her mid forties. I knew after the first few minutes that she would never finish the job on this hairy man that was I. After about twenty minutes, she called for help and was joined by another nurse in her late twenties. Together they smoothed me off in about 50 minutes.

Being shaved was the beginning of the end of me. Every bit of me except my head – yes even my scrotum – was pared smooth. So dangerously delicate my heart aneurysm was deemed that I was already confined to lying prone in bed. It was in this prone position that my hair got stripped. Intellectually, I knew why it was being done – hairs harbour germs – the chest must be totally clear – and the legs and arms, all four possible sites for harvesting veins for the bypasses. The groin yes, maybe a catheter would be needed some time. Why the scrotum? I still wonder at that.

Somehow it seemed, subjectively though, that I was being prepared for death or for sacrifice. Then I was thinking literally, physically. Little did I know that weeks and months later I would feel existentially, spiritually, metaphysically that I had been sacrificed and killed.

On the night of April 25, my family and intimates were permitted to stay well beyond the end of visiting hours. The de-hairing was not complete until about 9 pm and that was done in privacy – just me and the nurses. But with the ordeal of the operation next morning, it was thought I needed a good night's sleep so I was given a sedative. As it began to take, my family and intimates came to say good night and take their leave.

Alone and drowsy, I looked at my arms. Whose arms? They were not mine. They looked like the arms of a Japanese man – all smooth. I lifted the sheet and blanket to peer down my chest. My body was no longer mine. I was not my body. An alien had taken my place, and this was but a minor beginning.

In the Bible story, the patriarch Jacob drapes himself with goatskin to pose as his elder, hairy brother Esau, the rightful heir, thus deceiving his blind and dying father Isaac into leaving him the family fortune. In this verbal outpouring, I feel like the hairy brother Esau. My identity has been stolen, not by a wheeler-dealer younger brother, but as the emotional consequence of undergoing a full body shave. Not some big deal in itself, but the symbolic beginning of dramatic changes.

I have always been super-conscious of identity. Probably even a bit obsessive. From a ten-year old schoolboy to this day, questions such as Who am I? What should I become? Why am I here? What is this 'thing' I call 'I'? have fascinated me.

Before we had ballpoint pens, I remember sitting at my primary school desk, dipping a nibbed pen into the desk's drop-in ceramic inkwell, and writing:

> *Bruce Winston Wilson,*
> *42 Second Avenue,*
> *Campsie,*
> *Sydney,*
> *New South Wales,*
> *Australia,*

> *The Southern Hemisphere,*
> *The Earth,*
> *The Solar System,*
> *The Universe.*

In my late twenties, while working as a full-time chaplain at the University of New South Wales, I completed a social science degree. My honours thesis examined the processes by which each of us becomes a self, a person; explored the psycho-social construction of our '**I**,' '**me**' and '**thou**' identities. Then in my early sixties, after leaving active ministry as a bishop, I started up a face-to-face, one-to-one ministry of *Psycho-Spiritual Guidance for Church Leaders*. Helping leaders to understand themselves in relation to others, including the Divine. Over the years, I've learnt that whatever else it is, identity is a work in progress. But nothing had prepared me for the effect on my identity of living for many weeks under the hovering presence of death.

For weeks after I am home, the full body shave haunts me as a recurring flash-back. I am disturbed that I am so disturbed by it. Of itself it seems so trivial. My reaction makes me feel a bit of a sook.

Clearly, it's not a physical trauma. I shave my face every day. And my body hair will grow back after just a few weeks. Turning the spotlight on shaving of the scrotum makes me feel especially vulnerable – in the eyes of others and in my own eyes too. Open to the wildest Freudian, psychoanalytical interpretations of my identity crisis.

LIBIDO RATING

Except for a bit of temporary embarrassment at having a female stranger touch my intimate parts, I know that the sexual dimension of the actual shaving is pretty minor. But after some weeks of recuperation, it becomes clearer and clearer that my sexual identity itself has changed forever. Sexually I am no longer me. My old sexual self has died. The shaving marked the start of this. And this is hardly a trivial matter.

If asked for a libido score out of ten, where ten is the highest and zero the lowest, then before my heart attack I would rate myself a seven or an eight. Pretending at being a macho-man, I probably would have aspired to say 'Nine'. But factually I was already in my mid-sixties and, unbeknown, had a ninety per cent blockage in a heart artery. Ask me the same question at home after all my heart troubles, and I now rate myself between a one and a one and a half. And that rating applies still to this day.

Has this affected my sense of who I am, my identity? My maleness? Myself as a lover? My erotic joy? Yes, of course, hugely! Hugely!

In terms of purely physical performance, the diminishment is the result not just of my damaged heart and permanent heart arrhythmias but also of the drugs - especially the Beta-Blockers - that control the arrhythmias and keep me alive. These drugs are designed to dampen down feelings. To suppress glandular responses such as adrenaline rushes. They effectively diminish actual sexual feeling and desire, not just physical competence. It's chemical castration.

The full body shave marks the start of a physical transformation that saves my biological life but totally transforms my psychosexual identity. Sexually, I am no longer the 'me' I have been since puberty. Sexually, '**an alien**' has indeed taken my place and the 'I' I knew as '**me**' is dead. Flash-backs make it feel as if the shaving was ritual preparation. Preparation for a psycho-sexual, altar-sacrifice.

This is a transformation I needed to assimilate within a new sense of identity. Or else fall into the depths of despair and self-pity. A process assisted, above absolutely everything else, by admitting truthfully and self-honestly the reality and dimensions of my unwelcome metamorphosis. Applying to myself Freud's 'talking cure'. In other words, being real not false with myself. The 'getting a handle' scribblings certainly help do that. And discovering more deeply the value of intimate affection helped a lot too. It is a rocky road to travel though!

(My experience is **not** typical of those who've had 'normal' open-heart bypass surgery. In my case, bypass grafting was just an add-on extra – something that was possible to do – included with surgery for the more urgent matter of the pseudo-aneurysm. The sexuality of most bypass patients, due to improved heart function, is likely to be enhanced not diminished.)

LOSING THE HE-MAN

Not permitted to drive for many weeks, Zandra took me to Katoomba hospital heart rehab regularly. Here I began to meet a lot of men and women who'd been through experiences similar to mine. And much worse experiences! After his open-heart surgery, one guy had got a staph infection in his staple-repaired sternum. Bit by bit, over several months, his infected sternum was surgically removed. His ribs now floated around, unanchored in his central chest.

At rehab, I encountered a bloke who was about the angriest person I had ever met. He greeted others, if at all, with a grunt. He constantly voiced outrageous racist and sexist remarks to all around. Female rehab patients avoided him. He boasted of emptying local cafes of Asian tourists with his angry rants against those he called 'slit-eyes'. He made himself out to be caveman tough. The only explanation for his behaviour was some sort of deeply embedded emotional pain. My long pastoral-care experience, but more importantly the fresh loss of my own he-man identity, made me want to reach out to him.

Maybe referring to myself as having a he-man identity is a bit over the top. But since adolescence, I had always been a tall, muscular male, viewing myself as a physically strong man. At age 65, as mentioned earlier, just before my heart attack, I had been swinging a pick and wielding a shovel for hours on end. Creating wide, deep holes for planting fruit trees and long hedges at the newly purchased Leura property.

Nowadays, since heart surgery, I am a physical shadow of my former self. When gardening, I am only able to use small handtools. And my limit is about 45 minutes. Planting a new tree or shrub that once took twenty minutes now takes two hours. Being shaved became etched on my psyche as *'the beginning of the end'* of this physical *'me'*. *'No one told me though 'if you have this operation and live you – the you that you know is you –*

will be dead when it is all over'. Viewed in hindsight, it is the physical strength of masculine gender – with maybe a degree or two of macho-man posturing – that I felt was being prepared for sacrifice by the passively endured shaving.

Eventually, all of us have to accommodate loss of physical agency into our self-image. If nothing else, old age will see to that. The stage when, as Germaine Greer has said, the bits stop working or start falling off. Which is why we elderly say 'old age is not for wimps'.

Serious illness hastens physical decline. Eliminating normal stages of psycho-spiritual adjustment to slow bodily changes. Post heart attack, I become internally furious when mass media highlight the story of some eighty-year-old or other who has just climbed Mount Kosciuskzo, or swum the English Channel, or ran the New York marathon. As if this is typical rather than absolutely extraordinary! It is some seriously psychic denial of inevitable - and universal -physical decline. A media fantasy! Perhaps a Baby-Boomer fantasy?

Eventually – it took about one year – I earned the trust of the sexist, racist, angry bloke. I saw him weekly at hospital heart rehab. It turned out he had been a senior Australian army officer with actual combat experience in Vietnam. And that he had been orphaned in another country as a small child. Institutionalised, and eventually adopted out to strangers. (Who were good to him.) There was a lot more, but this was enough to begin to explain his atrocious and outrageous acting-out.

Throughout life, in his own mind, he was an invincible He-Man. A He-Man who had conquered all the personal challenges – wrestled-down all the demons –life had thrown at him (including Vietcong soldiers). But a heart attack, resulting in multiple stentings, had sapped away two-thirds and more of his physical abilities. Physically, he was a broken-man. And the world and everything in it was going to pay for that!

As with sexuality, self-honestly confronting reality is the beginning of wisdom. And of soul-healing. (Self-application of the Freudian talking cure.) A famous teaching of Jesus is *'the truth shall make you free'*. Another is *'When the Spirit of truth comes, he will guide you into all truth'*.

Appropriating a contented 'seniors' – or 'physically debilitated' – identity should be characterised by impressive psycho-spiritual, rather than bodily, feats. Dealing with the neglected demons of our early and middle life – and with the demons of haunting illness – is more challenging and more life-giving than chasing athletic triumphs. The broken He-Man had to tell his story to a listener. More importantly, he had to tell it to himself. But until he did tell it, there was no story – just anger and confusion.

This angry bloke – never my client or my parishioner, just a rehab mate –has become a close friend: at relative peace with himself and the Lifeworld. A generous financial supporter of the afflicted at home and overseas. A very nasty demon that tried to destroy him was a Vietnam War demon. Not the demon of what happened to him in Vietnam. Not the demon of what he saw there. The demon of what he did there. All the current popular discussion about Post Traumatic Syndrome Disorder seems to have it the other way around, misleadingly in my opinion.

Depression and Anxiety

Carl Jung says that if in the second half of life we don't deal with the problems that we've repressed in the first half of life, we are destined to go mad. Modern Western culture is not renowned for its pursuit of psycho-spiritual maturity – the Jungian remedy. That neglect goes a long way towards explaining its epidemics of depression and anxiety. Instead of wrestling with psycho-spiritual growth, personal, social – even spiritual – problems are regarded as medical issues of the brain. And treated with drugs. We can only get the right answers if we ask the right questions. Sometimes, it is very painful to ask the right questions, individually and socially. Is it because suddenly something has gone wrong with brains that our culture is suffering from epidemics of depression, anxiety, and suicide? An ironic question!

UNDER-THE-BUS SYNDROME

Being informed that my chance of survival was 50-50, it is unsurprising that I experienced the shaving – metaphorically – as ritual preparation for a sacrificial death. (My son disputes my constant reference to 50-50. He says he heard the young surgeon, Bill Lyons, pronounce more pessimistic odds: 60-40 against. And that I am putting a more positive spin on it.) Of course, mentally and intellectually, I already knew that I was mortal. My heart attack converted mere head knowing into body knowing.

Memory of the shaving haunted me because it marked my existential, physical awareness of death:

'Somehow it seemed, subjectively though, that I was being prepared for death or for sacrifice. Then I was thinking literally, physically. Little did I know that weeks and months later, I would

feel existentially, spiritually, metaphysically that I had been sacrificed and killed.'

In my headspace, I am part of the 'Baby Boomer scene'. I understand rebellion against the moral and spiritual confines – especially the sexual repression and the religious dogmatism - of our parent generation. I happily enjoy the fruits of Boomer rebellion. But I have huge difficulty accepting Boomer rebellion that now extends into middle age. Into retirement and even into old age itself. Since contracting a severe case of 'Under-The-Bus Syndrome', I want to scream out, **'Grow up!', 'Wake up!', 'Get your act together!'**.

John Leaney is an Adjunct Professor at University of Technology, Sydney. John and I first met at the University of NSW in 1970. He was a final year electrical engineering student and President of the Student Christian Union. I was the newly appointed – very young – full-time Anglican university chaplain. We remained friends for many years but gradually lost contact as our lives went in different directions, professionally and geographically. Many months into my recovery, almost by accident, we discovered that we lived 40 houses apart on the same side of the same street in Leura. We also discovered that we were both recovering from illness-induced, prolonged near-death experiences. John's was from leukaemia. Repeated bouts.

This created a new bond of understanding as we resumed the old friendship between us. We talked deeply, trying to understand each other's transformed identity. And our new ways of living and being and coping in the world. There was great mutual comfort as we realised how easily each understood what the other had gone – and was going – through. We found extreme difficulty discovering adequate words to explain this to family and friends who – lucky for them – had not had a similar experience. This disturbed us, so we kept trying.

We all know that life is uncertain. In conversation about future plans we often express this tritely and semi-jokingly - without any real sense of impending doom - as *'Who knows I could go under a bus tomorrow?'* But that does express -rather literally - how John and I have come to feel about the delicate contingency of life. My best attempt at putting in into words is this:

> 'I've been under the bus and under the bus and under the bus. And I'm just in front of the bus again now and every now. My old identity took for granted the plans of today and tomorrow and next year. But it was sacrificed and killed under the bus. My new identity knows a metaphysic of life's contingency that is existential, spiritual and, compared with the old identity, not upside-down but right way up. Thus much richer, deeper and more joyful.'

Boomer rebellion mocks and rejects its own rich spiritual tradition - the church (with all its faults but blessings too) and two millennia of the spirituality, art, philosophy and theology arising from the life and teachings of Jesus of Nazareth. It rejects – yet now barely even knows – the Big Story of the Bible and the great Christian Dreaming that unfolds out of it. Think, say, this tiny sample –Polycarp, Augustine, Hildegard, St Francis,

Bach, Tolstoy, Dostoyevsky, Bonhoeffer, Weil, Mother Theresa. Driven by capitalistic greed for material profits, seduced by psychologically trained marketeers and advertisers, Boomer rebellion has adopted instead a creed of consumer hedonism. Spiritually passing on to its own thoughtful – better educated – offspring nothing more than a conformist, almost entirely ignorant shallow atheism. Or a secularist nothingness.

A Parable Told By Jesus

And he said to them, "Take care! Be on your guard against all kinds of greed; for one's life does not consist in the abundance of possessions". Then he told them a parable: "The land of a rich man produced abundantly. And he thought to himself, 'What should I do, for I have no place to store my crops?' Then he said, 'I will do this: I will pull down my barns and build larger ones, and there I will store all my grain and my goods. And I will say to my soul, Soul, you have ample goods laid up for many years; relax, eat, drink, be merry'. But God said to him, 'You fool! This very night your life is being demanded of you. And the things you have prepared, whose will they be?' So it is with those who store up treasures for themselves but are not rich toward God."

THE JOY OF BEING WRONG

I said that, compared with my old identity, my new Under-The-Bus identity *is not upside-down but right way up. Thus much richer, deeper and more joyful.* Right way up! Richer! Deeper! More joyful! How can this be? It seems crazy!

Explaining this paradox puts me in danger of alienating all my readers - Secularist, Atheist, Christian, Agnostic, etc. Because I have monumental difficulty explaining a post-heart-troubles personal transformation that is vulnerable to terrible misunderstanding. Yet greatly treasured by me. Even with some very close friends, my attempts have been met with blank, bemused, if not semi-pitying, stares. Just what is he on about? Big deal, eh! So I need to supply a bit of background about my spiritual life.

I am not and have never been a guilt-tripper or guilt-wallower Christian. I am thankful that in neither family nor in school – neither as a child nor as an adolescent - was I subjected to any of those guilt-inducing Protestant or Catholic forms of Christianity that torment people for life. Paradoxically, I am thankful that as I grew up my father was an atheist, my mother only a nominal – occasionally Christmas or Easter - Christian. Thankful, too, that I was sent to state secular schools. The only psycho-spiritual influence on me – from my late teens – was the Anglican Church. And through her, I learnt love not fear, forgiveness not judgment, realism not fantasy.

Rationalist critics of Christianity frequently attack Anglicanism as intellectually soppy. Because it doesn't provide them with easy knockdown – 'man-of-straw' – authoritarian dogmas or self-righteous moralising. The Anglican Church self-consciously defines itself as a *via media* – a middle way between Protestant and Roman Catholic. It makes no claim to exclusive truth. Sees itself as only one part of the church founded by Jesus of Nazareth. It has no special theology of its own. Just the mainstream traditional orthodoxy of the Church both East and West – what most Christians have believed and practised all of the time.

My Anglican induction into the 'Way of Jesus' – via a very ordinary suburban church in a working-class, Sydney suburb – made it quite clear to me that, along with the whole human race, I am a self-centred and rivalrous being. A fact so obvious that I needed no convincing. Healthy realism. To use the traditional term, I share in Original Sin. A solidarity in egoism and narcissism with the whole human race. AS G.K. Chesterton once joked – 'the only empirically provable theological doctrine'.

I came to understand that a sense of God's absence – at its extremes, intellectual atheism or suicidal nihilism – is not a matter only of reason and intellect but also of will and conscience, of good and evil. That is to say, knowing God is a moral as well as an intellectual question. So it became clear that as well as seeking to understand God with my mind, I should also repent and confess my wrong doings, shortcomings and evil imaginings. **But with no need to wallow in them.**

I learnt and accepted that at the core of Jesus' life – key to all his words and works – is Divine grace. That we are 'saved' through God's love (grace) not by any intellectual, mental, moral or spiritual achievements (works) of our own. In simple terms, and it's best kept simple, God loves and accepts us in spite of our sins and in spite of our doubts. We are saved from the destructive, nihilistic effects of our sins – from our rivalrous, vengeful egoism – by grace. Saved by Divine love. Not by wallowing. Not by good works. That the world – us too – ends not with a bang or a whimper but with recreating Divine love.

This was the settled psycho-spiritual space occupied by my pre-'Under-The-Bus' identity. So it came as a huge shock when my post 'Under-The-Bus' identity gave this settled space an earthquake-type shaking.

I saw myself as having become complaisant about my spiritual and moral life. Caught up unawares, for example, in parts of the Boomer rebellion I should have questioned or shied away from. My heart attack had done for me what the grim conditions of a Siberian prison had done for the great Russian novelist Fyodor Dostoyevsky.

In **House of the Dead** – a slightly fictionalised account of his internment for political rebellion – he says '*In my spiritual solitude, I reviewed all my past life, went over it all to the smallest detail… judged myself sternly and relentlessly, and even sometimes blessed fate for sending me this solitude, without which I would not have judged myself like this, nor viewed my past so sternly*'.

One effect of the secularist tsunami I wrote about in Part One is the rejection of the whole idea of sin and guilt as old-fashioned, sick, or as the tool of manipulating priests. Epitomised, for example, by public figures, who when caught out – with white powder up their noses, or their pants down, or their hands in the till, or telling blatant lies – do not confess to acting wrongly or evilly, but only to making a mistake. Or when they use the weasel-word apology **not** 'I am sorry I hurt you' **but rather** 'I am sorry that you feel hurt'. Meaning that 'It's your problem, not mine'. Much modern psychological and psychiatric theory, too, frequently replaces the ethical categories of sin, selfishness, narcissism, rivalry, envy and guilt with inappropriate categories drawn from medicine such as psychopathological, sick, ill, abnormal, injured.

As I said, I find all this hard to explain even to my friends. You could call it the joy of being wrong.

As it seems for Dostoyevsky, I became more and more aware of specific acts of selfishness. Of rivalry, of nasty things done and said. Aware too of actions of care, kindness and social justice left undone that should have been done. **They emerged as active memories not abstract notions. Some with visualisation.** The girlfriend I dropped callously without explanation. The terminally ill priest I failed to keep in touch with after he retired. The grieving father I – being too busy – failed to comfort properly after his wife, my mother, died. The immigrant student at college I'd verbally bullied and ganged up against. The colleague I'd ridiculed behind his back but charmed face-to-face in order to win his vote. The worthy charity to which I donate less because it doesn't have tax deductibility. Hundreds and hundreds of unconfessed and therefore unresolved sins rose into vivid self- awareness. I had had no idea!

But! But!

But – and I cannot stress this strongly enough – this was a positive, joyful metamorphosis. Devoid of torment or wallowing. It was the joy of being wrong. That this seems so counter-intuitive is probably the reason I find it extremely difficult to explain.

It was like a healing: ridding me of spiritual, polluting junk. More accurately, it was like being cured of an underlying, enervating chronic disease that I didn't even know I had. I cannot find adequate words. It was welcome, elating. It was grace upon grace. It caused in me new feelings of compassion towards others, towards all creatures and towards nature herself. It was as though they all became part of me and I of them. It was like a foretaste of heaven. A preparation for the Age-To-Come. It was 'Bless you heart attack for being in my life'.

I can easily imagine that if I had physically died in April-May 2008, I would still need to have been drawn by Divine grace along this same purging path.

Heaven

Part of the Big Story is the reality and hope of heaven. Orthodox Christians, East and West, don't believe – as so many of the new fashionista or fundamentalist atheists seem to think we should believe – that heaven is up in the sky. Or in the outer realms of deep space. Both the sky and deep space are part of creation. God is not any sort of 'thing' in God's own creation. Eastern Orthodox iconography depicts the sky blue and heaven gold, marking the difference. In the Biblical New Testament, heaven is pictured in categories of time not space. Our world is 'this present age', sometimes 'this present evil age'. Heaven is the life of the 'Age-To-Come', the 'new creation'. In the words of the creed repeated in Christian churches weekly at worship all over the world '... *we look for the resurrection of the dead and the life of the world to come*'. The Lord's Prayer or Our Father – the prayer that Jesus taught his followers to pray, iterated millions and millions of times in every imaginable language across the globe daily – says, addressing God, '... *thy kingdom come, thy will be done in earth as in heaven...*'

PITS AND CHOICES

About six weeks after getting home, I am in the deepest pits, feeling more dead than alive. I am not recovering and never will recover the way a heart bypass patient might expect to recover. My heart has suffered irreparable damage – scar tissue from the actual heart attack, the effects of a sewn-in patch repair and jumbled electrics. I've started trying to explain how it feels via a motoring analogy – *'It's like a throbbing, powerful, Ford V8 car engine has been swapped-over for a whining, little, two-stroke Vespa scooter engine that backfires intermittingly'.*

I am taking Digoxin (from the foxglove plant), which increases the power of my weak heart but causes extreme loss of appetite and 24/7 nausea, with vomiting and diarrhoea. I am feeling I made the wrong choice. Feeling that maybe I was meant to die and that, perversely, the choice to live was disastrous. Here is a bit of what I wrote, unedited, pouring out feelings, attempting to climb out of this emotional sorry-pit:

I had agreed in haste to take this downward journey. Looking back, I wonder if I chose it at all, or drifted into it for the sake of others. Zandra and the family were there. Perhaps they chose it. Perhaps I chose it for them.
"If you don't have the operation, you will be dead in a few days." That is what the seriously smiling young surgeon, lounging at the end of the bed in jeans and a cheap T-shirt, pronounced. 'And what about the surgery? What's the chance of surviving that?' " 50-50 but I can't be more precise than that."
Sounds dangerous, I say – 'Yes, very dangerous', says the surgeon, 'but you have no option, without it you'll be dead in a day or two.'

'There is an aneurysm in the right wall of your heart, the wall has developed a bubble, a balloon, it's very thin – the only thing preventing it from bursting is the tissue around it is inflamed and swollen.'

Mind pictures: the balloon bursts but blood not air rushes out, filling the chest cavity, oozing from mouth and nose, bright red, scarletted against blue lips and face.

'You have no choice.' It did seem that way. The 'decision' was made that way – no choice. So, the logic is, the reason is death or life, it's no choice.

A *'downward journey'* is a good descriptor of the wasted, enervated, weak, nauseated condition I was in. The issue confronted is – 'If I'd known that I'd feel like this, would I have chosen the surgery?' Wrong choice! Yes? No?

The previous day, I had gone back to Westmead Hospital for an early check-up. A nurse casually mentioned that my heart had actually burst in the surgeon's hands. She thought I already knew this. I didn't. (Zandra thought she'd told me, maybe she had, but I had no recollection.) There and then, I fell into tears and was inconsolable most of the long drive back home to Mt Victoria. I could not explain why? Maybe I had body memory of the operation. I just felt so vulnerable. The lurid and melodramatic detail I draw on – **Mind pictures: the balloon bursts but blood not air rushes out** – ups the stakes of the choice dilemma. In my vivid imagination, the operation is a failure – the patient, me, is dying. Wrong choice!

Body Memory

Maybe, and this is entirely speculative, post-surgery our bodies remember what happened to them even though our brain's conscious centres are shut down. I have discussed this at length with a psychotherapist friend who considers it a plausible way of understanding post-operative trauma. It is a bit like some car accident victims. They go into deep shock and have no memory of the accident afterwards. The intentional injury inflicted by invasive surgery, though carefully controlled, is not unlike major injury caused by motoring accidents. A very large part of our human functioning is – unawares to consciousness – controlled by our autonomous nervous system. So it would not be surprising that the body has its own, unconscious 'memories' of physical assault, whatever the cause. Body memory rather than brain memory. Unconscious memory rather than conscious memory. Maybe someday research will negate or confirm this hypothesis. Post-operative trauma is certainly real, whether mental or physical, psychic or somatic.

OPTIONS

As mentioned earlier, about this same time, my psychiatrist friend John Hoskyn came to visit. He asked me exactly the question 'Did you choose to have the invasive surgery?' It seemed a pretty brutal ask. Out of character too – normally John is a gentle person. It shocked me.

I am fairly sure that John, seeing my low physical state and skeletal body - knowing as only a medico can know just what a risky procedure I'd undergone, and what nasty complications might follow – was pretty certain I'd made the wrong choice.

I knew that behind his question was recent memory of a close, mutual friend whose family, especially his medical-professional daughter, had persuaded him into having surgery. Surgery that did nothing but make the last months of his life hell on earth. Soon, our mutual friend made a different, new, courageous choice. Desiring, in his own words, 'to sink peacefully behind the velvet curtain', he refused further treatment and died. I think John was concerned that I was following the same path. He couldn't hide his concern.

For me, John opened a can of worms, both very practical and very deeply philosophical. Are we condemned to freedom with no meaning outside ourselves, as Jean Paul Sartre would say? Is freedom just a word for nothing left to lose – and perhaps a justification for choosing suicide not life – as Janis Joplin once sang? Or is freedom the supreme gift of God? The transcendence that separates us from all other known creatures? The grace by which to know as well as to be known by God? Is choice a burden? – definitely 'Yes'. But a burden worth the cost of being human?

When we are diagnosed with a terminal illness, as I was, and are offered an invasive surgical or medical solution, we have to weigh up whether it will be worth it or not. Will our quality of life after the intervention be good enough to justify the ordeals caused by the intervention? Or will our quality of life be so poor that we will wish we allowed the illness to take its course? How do we know? Well, we should try to find out, shouldn't we?

Currently, we tend not to face these options until excessive treatment, via umpteen 'life-saving' interventions, leaves us

– or a loved one – with unbearable suffering. At which point frequently, it's the 'Universe' ('I don't deserve this') or God ('How could a loving God allow…') who gets the blame. Irrationally, undeservedly, but understandably.

To adopt the hard, non-euphemistic language we use in the case of our companion animals, such intensity of suffering opens up debate about whether the sufferers should be 'put down' or 'put to sleep' via assisted suicide. This is far too big an issue to open up here. But some years ago, with Cardinal Ted Clancy – then the Roman Catholic Archbishop of Sydney – I had the task of drawing up a statement on euthanasia for release by the National Council of Churches. We made a clear distinction between active euthanasia (putting down) and passive euthanasia (withdrawal of futile treatment, allowing death to take its natural course). We thought active euthanasia violated the infinite value of each person. We thought excessive and futile treatment violated it too. Oops, I have probably opened up the subject too much already. It is a huge topic.

Printed accounts from my health insurance company started arriving in the mail. I began calculating the all-up costs of my hospital treatment. Including payments to twenty-four doctors and the cost of the defibrillator, the bills were in excess of $A100,000.00. I was staggered by the sum. It's not what it cost me personally. It includes all the costs paid by my insurer and by the taxpayers of Australia via government-funded Medicare rebates. But it provoked another set of serious questions about choices and options.

At a personal level, I felt some 'survivor guilt'. I added to what I wrote about choices that day – *Why should an old bloke like me have all these community resources spent on him when the same amount of money could save the lives of several hundred small children in poor countries? I am already past the age when I can give of my best.*

This is too big a problem for individuals to solve! And writing this down made me feel worse. But along with all the mainstream Australian churches –together with charities such as World Vision and Doctors Without Borders (MSF) – we can pressure our Government to lift support for overseas aid. For my little individual part, I transformed some of my 'survivor guilt' into digging deeper-down into my pockets for charities such as I've mentioned, and for others such as Save The Children.

The staggering bills raised an issue closer to home. Just because modern scientific medicine can – is able and competent – to perform a procedure, should it? This is an issue of urgency. New technologies already outstrip our ethical, social and spiritual understanding. And where do we draw the line when spending the health dollar? With an ageing population, Australia is faced with an intergenerational ethical problem. Is there a calculus for rational, humane, ethical health-spend limits based on life expectancy? Already we know that it costs huge sums of money to keep us elderly alive – in ICUs – for a few extra weeks before the end. Money well spent?

'*Yes, very dangerous*', says the surgeon, '*but you have no option, without it you'll be dead in a day or two.*'

After Bill Lyon's bedside pronouncement, I have no memory of giving any consideration to possible outcomes other than dead or alive. What type of alive was not discussed. In my case, the very short time between diagnosis and possible urgent surgical intervention hardly allowed for it. All deep philosophical questions aside, I think that's why the choice question became so big in my head later.

Now I am home, the suffering-in-the-pits 'me' that is actually alive has come to think that the 'me' who 'chose' surgery might more wisely have chosen death. So who can I blame? Someone must have made me make the wrong choice? From what I wrote (see above), I am out to find a scapegoat. Someone to blame for my misery. Bill Lyons? The family? Zandra? With hindsight, how incredibly embarrassing! Yet how humanly normal.

In the Biblical story of Adam and Eve – one of the most profound stories ever told – Adam and Eve may choose to eat fruit from any tree in the Garden of Eden except the tree that is in the *middle* of the garden (nothing about apples here). God forbids eating fruit from the Middle Tree, saying it would result in human creatures becoming like God – conscious, with eyes open, knowing the difference between good and evil. Tempted by the wily serpent, Eve, the stronger character, eats the fruit of the Middle Tree. She gives some to Adam. He meekly follows her lead and eats too. Immediately, they discover they have not become like God at all. Instead, as attempted usurpers they have fallen from paradise. Fallen into death-aware, self-consciousness. Fallen into rivalrous – and sexually charged -mutual separation. (Fallenness soon results in the greatest of evils. Their elder son

Cain murders his younger brother Abel). As the cause of the disaster, Eve blames the serpent and Adam blames Eve. Neither accepts responsibility for their own choice. A perfect description in my mind of the human condition. And of my own solidarity in it.

Adam and Eve

Words from a talk by John Dominic Crossan, Biblical scholar:

'My point… is not that those ancient people told literal stories and we are now clever enough to take them symbolically, but that they told them symbolically and we are now dumb enough to take them literally'.

Absurdly, in the pits, I was looking around for someone to blame. Who is it who coerced me into this enervation and decrepitude? This 24/7 nausea? My most stupid denunciation is against Bill Lyons, bitterly now described namelessly as *'the seriously smiling young surgeon, lounging at the end of the bed in jeans and a cheap T-shirt'*. Why is he to blame? Because it has to be someone else's fault and he told me that I had no choice – *'you have no option'.*

Zandra and the family were there. Perhaps they chose it. Perhaps I chose it for them.

At death's door a loving family will want their afflicted loved one saved. This puts pressure on choice. It led to John Hoskyn's friend and mine making a disastrous choice. His daughter could not let him go in spite of the terrible suffering he was enduring. Had that happened to me? Could I blame Zandra and the family making me feel this bad? Had they clung onto me? Why shouldn't they?

It took some weeks plus slightly better health but by venting my distress, angrily, with written accusation and blame, I worked through to accepting that I did choose my circumstances. Bitter as I then felt about them. Like Adam and Eve I could not fool God – the deepest Truth – about my personal responsibility.

It may sound a bit arrogant or self-deluded but I believe it was a choice I made not just for myself but also for others. A quick death was going to leave behind a lot of mess: nothing was prepared, not even a proper will. I was distressed at the housing and financial mess I would leave for Zandra. Mt Vic unsold, Leura half- moved-into. If I lived – as became the case – I knew that I had a lot of practical loving to get on with for the sake of these others. I also felt that whatever suffering I faced, God would support me.

Yes, it's all a bit of a First World problem for sure. That relativises it. Gives it perspective you don't see when you're in it. But it doesn't lessen the suffering or the struggle. And this First World problem throws up huge ethical, philosophical, and spiritual issues that are pressing and universal.

But what about that bloody doctor who failed to diagnose my original heart attack? He deserves blame! He really deserves it. He himself deserves to suffer, doesn't he?

THAT DOCTOR -RAGE AND REVENGE

My feelings about Dr Qem loomed large in me. Stalked by inward anger and malevolent desire for vengeance.

For years, I have studied the demanding writings of a French-American genius Rene Girard, founder of interdividual (*sic*) mimetic psychology. Girard demonstrates that at core our human relationships tend to be steeped in rivalry and violence. Verbally or physically, if someone hurts us, we strike back. Then they strike back. Then we strike back again, etc. We become, says Girard, indistinguishable doubles. Each always blaming the other for starting it. Each believing they are an innocent victim of a nasty troublemaker. These rivalrous cycles are only broken by serious physical or emotional violence. Or by mediated compromises. Or by court orders. Or when one side turns the other cheek.

I am emotionally conflicted about Dr Qem. A victim of the enormous consequences of his simple negligence. But nightly news reports of the sufferings and injustices in the wider world expose my situation as just another old bloke's 'First World Problem'. 'Get over it!' would be relevant advice. Easy to say, but how? My head is still full of it. I started with my usual tack, pouring out feelings on paper, including this time a heading –

THE INCOMPETENT DR

It's the shoulder that dislocated in 1964. Marked the end of a not very glorious rugby union career. The Anglicans versus the Baptists it was – Moore College XV against the Baptist College XV. It was a tackle that prevented a certain Baptist try, there was glory there. And what a welcome back in the dining hall that night, shoulder strapped up. But the pain, worst ever – until now. Same shoulder, as I said – 2008, forty-four years later. What could it be? That new house – planting the hedges, the fruit trees, the gums, the deciduous. Day after day, wielding the pick, the mattock, the shovel. Feeling so good, so strong. The pain, the shoulder, so severe that I am the pain. One in the morning, I woke with it. Is it bone pressing on a nerve, the old injury stirred up, jarred and jarred by breaking the hard ground of planting.

Well, Dr, I've been doing a lot of heavy gardening lately, swinging the pick into rocky ground, dislocated the shoulder in my twenties. Could it be a nerve-aggravated old injury?

About my age, Dad had a heart attack. Didn't know it at the time because no chest pain, only shoulder pain. Could I be having a heart attack, Dr?

"It's a bit of a mystery. You have free movement of the shoulder – pain does not increase or decrease as you rotate arm/shoulder. A mystery. My best guess is pleurisy. Got a cough? No! Hmm I'll give you some pain killers, anti-inflammatories and antibiotics. Pleurisy my best guess."

"Are you breathless? No! Well you are definitely not having a heart attack. Pleurisy the best guess."

No tests. No blood to take. What about an ECG, worth a guess. Silly old coot. Nerves pinched! Heart attack! As if the old footy injury could recall his glory days, make the pain meaningful. And just like Dad, eh! Interpret the present through the past, give continuity. A bit of pleurisy will burst those bubbles. Heart attack but not breathless.

Arrogant! Showed no compassion for pain at all. Told it was 9½ out of 10 pain. Didn't register a blink of feeling. A mystery, a bit of a mystery! Best guess. OK, we'll plunge a bet of pain killers, anti-inflammatories, antibiotics on pleurisy, running today as a twenty-five to one chance. He's racing.

I rehearse these now familiar past events in order to 'get a handle' on my inner fury. I am venting anger, wrestling with nasty emotions of rage, resentment and revenge. Profound and complex ethical issues! Is it just about professional performance? What about human weakness and error? It is profound and complex because the professional involved – a medical doctor – operates in the field of life and death. His neglect has taken me to death's door. Left me permanently debilitated. What can I do? What should I do? Is there anything I can do? Am I simply a victim? And there's a whispering voice saying, 'Is there contributory responsibility?'

Since my Qem consultation, I've learnt some things that give me the wisdom of hindsight. If Dr Qem had diagnosed the heart attack I endured across the desk from him in his consulting room, the proper procedure was to immediately administer aspirin, some nitrate spray/tablet to relieve the intense angina pain, and then call for an ambulance. In hospital, all that would probably have followed was an angiogram. The implanting of a single stent. A one or two-night stay.

There would be
- * no three weeks of post heart attack symptoms without treatment,
- * no pseudo-aneurysm,
- * no open-heart surgery,
- * no burst heart,
- * no Gortex patch,

* no EPS,
* no permanent Atrial Fibrillation,
* no frequent Ventricle Tachycardia,
* no intermittent Ventricle Fibrillation,
* no implanted defibrillator,
* no defibrillator electric shocks.

It might be a First World problem but it surely justifies an emotional response?

So – still sick as the proverbial dog – it is no surprise that I am raging with anger and bitterness towards Dr Qem. I bitterly and sarcastically compare his 'best guess' pleurisy diagnosis with a punter at the racecourse taking a pin to the form guide in order to decide which horse to bet on.

Best guess. OK we'll plunge a bet of pain killers, anti-inflammatories, antibiotics on pleurisy, running today as a twenty-five to one chance. He's racing.

And his manner is arrogant. He the knower talking down to me the ignoramus – that is how I felt. As I write this outpouring, I feel it more strongly now. I made very clear to him my continuous excruciating pain. I was folded into a foetal position in the chair in front of him – but he gave no flicker of concern or compassion. Expletives are exploding in my mind.

Yet there is a bit of ambivalence. It is not just an angry rave against Dr Qem. Given how ill I felt – and through grave neglect the serious damage Qem has caused me – that is surprising. I make a vague attempt to explore the possibility that I may have contributed to the misdiagnosis. I call myself a '**Silly Old Coot**'. And offer a diagnosis of my symptoms as the old-aged aggravation of an old rugby injury. *Well, Dr, I've been doing a lot* *of heavy gardening lately, swinging the pick into rocky ground, dislocated the shoulder in my twenties, could it be a nerve-aggravated old injury?*

By telling him about the footy injury and the recent heavy gardening, was I contributing to the misdiagnosis? Am I the victim or am I in danger of playing the victim?

By June 30th 2008 – twelve weeks after my one and only consultation with Dr Qem – I have firmly decided in favour of incompetence. His incompetence as a professional medical doctor. I have decided that I have not contributed to the misdiagnosis and far from making a simple mistake Qem is grossly negligent. And I need to do something about it.

By this time, I have become aware that the symptoms I described to him were such classic symptoms of a heart attack that the diagnosis would be run-of-the-mill for any registered nurse or doctor. To make matters worse, I asked him if I could have been having a heart attack and he said 'No'. And worst of all – he proposed no investigation. No blood tests. No electrocardiogram. The question I face is, 'What should I do about this bloody doctor?'

SUE FOR A MILLION DOLLARS

There are many days of gutted physical illness and emotional desolation when my answer is *'sue for a million dollars'*. At my angriest worst, I want to strike back at Qem – to make him pay for what I believe he has done to me. Become a Rene Girard revengeful, double – 'You did me, so now I am going to do you!' In other words 'an eye for an eye, a tooth for a tooth' – retributive justice – the very philosophy of vengeance that Jesus said should be replaced by 'turn the other cheek'.

Sue for a million dollars! I know people in similar circumstances who actually have. 'The love of money is the root of all evil', says the epistle to Timothy in the New Testament. An aphorism constantly misquoted to say that *money*, rather than *the love of money*, is the root of all evil. Love of money is idolatry: substituting our metaphysical desire for God with mundane desire for the goodies, the stuff and the social influence/prestige money can buy. (Dante says 'envy' is the root of all evil, an explication surely!) As a God-substitute, money never satisfies, no matter how much you get. Love of money installs self-love on a pedestal. Replacing love for one's neighbour with competitiveness, rivalry and exploitation.

At that mid-sixties stage of my life, chiefly through superannuation, savings, lucky investing and inheritance, I already have enough money to live on. After some deep, troubled wrestling with God about my motives, I decide that in my circumstances suing for money is nothing but lust for revenge. So still the question is, 'What should I do about this bloody doctor?'

What I do is submit a formal complaint about Qem to the appropriate Australian authority. That authority is the Commissioner of The Health Care Complaints Commission (HCCC) established by a 1993 Act of the New South Wales Parliament.

The HCCC pro forma asks me the question: **What do you want as a result of your complaint?** I respond: *That this doctor* should never make a similar mistake with other patients and to hear that he has acknowledged his errors in my case.

My vengeful feelings do not go away but I have striven to control them.

Irony of ironies! Through this complaints process, I discover that the man I am so angry with, the man my demons want to destroy, the man my angels want me to forgive, is a church-attending fellow Christian. Not that that makes any difference to what happened. His professional treatment should be the same for an atheist as for a co-religionist. Unprofessional medical neglect delivers an equal-opportunity outcome for theists and atheists. If I had known earlier on that Qem was a fellow Christian, it certainly would have affected my response. It would have made me even more incensed and angry about his neglect. And white-hot with fury about his lack of empathy.

To cut a long story short, through the proper complaints processes and via personal communications and 'phone conversations, I received this unamended letter from Dr Qem:

> Dear Rev Bruce Wilson,
>
> I am writing this letter to apologise for the provision of care that I provided in general practice on the 4th April 2008. When I first saw you on that day, I had noted that you had seen Dr Andrew Masterton the day before with what were gastrointestinal symptoms likely from a viral illness. When you presented with left shoulder pain I immediately thought that this was connected to the recent illness that may have triggered an

inflammatory shoulder pain. However I was wrong. Although it was not mentioned in the medical notes, I must have also dismissed your concerns to me that your father had a similar presentation of cardiac pain which you had explained to me during the consultation. You had explained that it was probably one of the worst shoulder pains but unfortunately, I continued to associate this with the recent illness. I note from the medical records that you must have had a myocardial infarction somewhere between 10/4/2008 and 22/4/2008 with a troponin T elevation and an ECG that suggested this upon presentation to Emergency department.

On hindsight and upon review of the medical notes, I suspected that on 4th April 2008 you presented with warning signs of cardiac pain which I had missed. At the least I should have probably performed an ECG to exclude cardiac ischemia. I apologise for this and I am sorry for this. I thank you that you have warned me about this error. I have since changed my practice, and I am now performing ECG on all patients who present with shoulder, left arm pain, chest pain, epigastric pain, neck pain, jaw pain in the hope that I will avoid making the same mistake again.

I am sincerely sorry and apologise for the pain that you may have suffered. I hope that even though I have made a professional mistake you can accept my apology. I pray that God continue to bless you in your work. If I can be of any help I may be contactable on the above.

Regards,
Dr Qem

Eight months after my heart attack, I am able to put the matters to rest by penning this unamended reply:

4 December, 2008
Dear Dr Qem,

I have received your letter dated 23rd November 2008 in which you apologise for your diagnostic and other errors in treating me following a consultation on April 4th this year. You also state that you have learnt from these errors and that they will make you more careful in your practise of medicine. Recognising that the errors have contributed greatly to my physical and mental suffering, and to that of my family and friends, as well as costing the state and my medical fund a lot of money, I accept your apology and entirely forgive you for making the errors. I wish you well in your ongoing medical career.

Yours Sincerely,
(Right Reverend Bruce Wilson)

A sign of some letting-go and my finding inward peace about the 'bloody doctor' is that I started to call him the **neglectful** rather than the **incompetent** doctor.

CHANCE OR PURPOSE?

The odds against my survival of the pseudo-aneurysm were huge. Lloyd Davis, before ever he knew anything about me personally – when I was just another anonymous patient handed over to him from Westmead Emergency – made two throwaway, unintentionally profound comments. On one bedside visit, he said, 'You've won Lotto; you know that, don't you?' At the time, I hadn't really taken it in that my odds were Lotto odds. I thought I'd just fallen on the good side of 50-50 survival predictions. A couple of days later, as he was going out the door of my hospital room, he turned to me, his index finger gesturing upward, and said 'Somebody up there must like you'.

To this day, I know nothing of Dr Davis' own philosophy, theology or spirituality. I am sure he intended nothing especially deep by his two comments. Statistically, they were factual. They were meant to buck up my spirits. But was my survival just a matter of chance? A one in a billion lucky draw out of the medical Lotto barrel? Or did a 'Somebody Up There' have something to do with it? If so, then what kind of a 'Somebody Up There' might that be?

After a few weeks at home, the extent of my 'good luck' finally sank in. I started taking these questions seriously. Of course, I had thought about such matters before. But escaping death by a whisker threw them into a new light. Confusingly!

Luck – the wheel of fortune – and providence – the guiding hand of God. Which applied? Not only about the momentous issue of survival, also about detail. For example, about the paradoxical 'good fortune' that the Mt Vic house had not sold.

A great blessing. This was the same big issue in little guise – chance or purpose? Probability or providence? Was 'Somebody Up There' really looking after me or was that just interpretive, pious rubbish in my head? To try to think clearer, as usual I put some thoughts and feelings on paper. I gave them the heading 'Mt Vic Providential?' -

By early May 2008, the Mt Vic house had been on the market for 7 months. It had not sold. I had dropped the price $35,000 and indicated I was open to lower offers. Nothing.

It was a bad time to sell – federal election, Christmas, interest rate rises.

It is a fabulous house in a fabulous location.

In the depth of illness, thinking if ever I was to live, leave hospital and go home, my total desire was to go to Mt Vic. I trembled in horror at the prospect of going to the new house in Leura. It was not yet home in any way. My intimates concurred, by my tears they knew how important Mt Vic would be. We talked, me in bed they around 3 sides. Isn't it wonderful Mt Vic hasn't sold, we said, and even further 'it's providential'.

Providential? Providential!

What kind of God would make sure a house had not sold because he knew it would be saving and comforting for a person who had an undiagnosed heart attack followed by horrific complications? A sadistic manipulator? A real God would surely have prevented the misdiagnosis or the heart attack in the first place!

Yes, that is what logic says. But emotion and intuition say 'It is providential that the house did not sell.'

The two positions are totally contradictory and both are true. Neither logic nor intuition can 'say' 'imbibe' (?) how.
F. Scott Fitzgerald – 'The test of a first-rate intelligence is the ability to hold two opposed ideas in the mind at the same time'.

The big issue was where for me was God – if at all – in these recent happenings? Now I was out of hospital and home at Mt Vic, could I make any sense of it all? Was that family hospital-bed talk about God and the sale of the Mt Vic house just sentimental rubbish? Was I fooling myself? If so, what then?

It is easy in many parts of our lives – especially in our romantic love-lives and in our private spiritual lives – to believe what we want to believe. To build castles in the air. But when we begin to take actual abode in these castles, we are in need of a good psychiatrist or priest – or some pretty serious reflection – to bring us back to earth. These meandering musings headed **Mt Vic Providential?** were more the cause than the result of deep reflection.

THIS IS TOO HARD

After completing a draft of this part of my story, I wanted to scrap the whole thing. As I repeated earlier, God for me is not an issue. I cannot even conceive that we humans are the top consciousness of the Lifeworld. It makes no sense. There has to be a higher self-conscious than us. A 'Most High' – one of the names for God in the Hebrew Bible (Old Testament). **But God's relationship to the Lifeworld – and me - is a great puzzle.** Baffling. Perplexing. A hugely complicated issue! Here, I see only tiny glimmers of light in a very deep, dark mystery. Yet it's worth trying to make as much sense as one can. Even if it's not much. So I forced myself to keep at it.

Years ago, a neurologist friend proposed that maybe God's relationship to the Lifeworld is like the relationship of our minds to our brain and bodies. I found that a bit helpful. But it does not make much sense of God's place in evil, sickness and death, does it? Anyway, with **Mt Vic Providential?** I was looking for help and comfort not theories. I was also looking for reality not self-fooling fantasy. That was the twist.

I have no idea how the F. Scott Fitzgerald quote got in my mind. I've read a couple of his novels, including **The Great Gatsby.** But this is from his essay *The Crack-Up* which I have never read. Maybe it was quote of the day on a desk calendar? In full it reads, 'The test of a first-rate intelligence is the ability to hold two opposed ideas in the mind at the same time, **and still retain the ability to function**'. He is talking about staying sane – not cracking-up – when plagued by inner psychic contradictions. In *Mt Vic Providential?* I am wrestling with Chance vs Providence – seeing truth in both. With my limited intelligence, trying to keep sane as I seek to understand God's role – if any – in my heart afflictions.

It seems quite nutty to hold that failure to sell a piece of real estate was due 1) to the caring hand of God and 2) to the conditions of the economy in general and the real estate market in particular. Emotionally, the crazy contradiction goes like this. On the one hand, my afflictions are caused by the inaction of a 'sadistic manipulator. *(A real God would surely have prevented the misdiagnosis or the heart attack in the first place!)*'. On the other hand, I am being tenderly cared for by a compassionate divine overseer. (*'Yes, that is what logic says. But emotion and intuition say it is providential that the house did not sell.'*)

Still today, I occupy this same, crazy, tough emotional paradox. I still face the Fitzgerald dilemma of acquiring *'... the ability to hold two opposed ideas in the mind at the same time, and still retain the ability to function'.* 'And still emotionally, it's just like Dr Davis saying one day that my survival was a Lotto win, and another day it was because somebody up there liked me. He was being folksy. But with time I've realised that, even for him, there is deep business behind his simple sayings. I can't precisely define what, but it has something to do with our desire to live in a meaningful, caring Lifeworld. So that even in face of suffering, sickness and death, we might sense meaning, not just randomness. *'Human beings can put up with almost anything so long as they can see a purpose in it'.* A saying of an American theologian that's stuck in my memory, though I can't recall his name.

Rationally, I do not believe that God intervened to prevent the sale of the Mt Victoria house for my convalescence' sake. If God had prevented it, then I might well blame God for the huge real estate downturn in Mt Victoria. That meant I had to lower the price by a massive $150,000 in order to sell it.

Along with all our educated ancestors of at least the past three thousand years, we know that God does not normally interfere in the regularities of nature. Even eras that were more open to the idea of miracles than ours prove this point. By definition, miracles are irregularities. But that God does not normally interfere, does not mean that God doesn't ever interfere, or that God cannot interfere. The possibility of miracles cannot be ruled out rationally. Indeed, in the light of what modern physics now knows – especially at the quantum level – we occupy a place of surprising – miraculous? – regularity.

Trivial interference, such as arranging the non-sale of an old bloke's house in a small village – even if the motive was compassion – makes the Most High look ridiculously like the Lifeworld's stage-magician. And if God did not perform equivalent little miracles for every ill and dying old bloke, then the Most High would look like a perverse and capricious Lifeworld stage-magician. Crazily, many religious, New Age, Fundamentalist and irrational people see God just like this. Talk about living in one's castles in the air!

I wanted and still do want to believe that there is Providence not just Lotto.

Everyone lives in a Big Story. It cannot be otherwise. Even if the Big Story is an anti-story. How we make sense – or cannot make sense – of our personal lives, especially our fears, sufferings and afflictions, depends on our Big Story. We all have a Big Story. As I've said, I occupy the Christian Big Story. Though for many people their Big Story is implicit not explicit. By answering just three questions, we can make our Big Story explicit:

* Where ultimately do we come from?
* How should we behave and why?
* Where does it all end up, us too?

There is no provable Big Story. At least not one that is beyond reasonable doubt. We do not have the omniscience necessary for that. So the question must be about plausibility: the preponderance of evidence. Does my Big Story best fit the facts of what I know and what I experience? Is it plausible? To choose to live in a particular Big Story is the act of faith the Danish philosopher Kierkegaard says is inescapable. Unavoidable except by self-deceit!

LOTTO ET CETERA

Lotto is definitely one plausible Big Story. One way of making sense of my heart troubles and afflictions. According to this story, they are the consequence of living in an impersonal, matter-energy world subject to decay (entropy) and randomness. It is, therefore, just good luck that the Mt Vic house hadn't sold and bad luck (a one in about one-hundred thousand chance) that the insertion of a coronary artery stent led to an aneurysm. And very, very good luck that the aneurysm occurred in a 20th century Western hospital equipped with modern medical technology and trained specialists.

This 'wheel of fortune', Lotto explanation **reads into** my personal experience a contestable metaphysical Big Story. Constructed by, and proselytised by, scientific materialists and philosophical atheists. A **reading into** based on a Big Story that says at core the Lifeworld – ontologically, its very Ground of Being – is random, impersonal matter-energy: it cares not a whit about the self-conscious, reasoning human creatures it has produced. By definition, it cannot – not merely does not. There is no conscious Creator of – or working in – the evolutionary cosmic and biological processes of life. They are only impersonal matter-energy processes. On this view, Providence is a joke.

Wishful fantasy. Those who believe in it are either irrational or to be pitied.

It is impossible to disprove the Lotto view, or to deny its rational plausibility, only to insist that it is an unproven **reading into.** There is no salvation in this Big Story. Only despair, or stoic acceptance or will-to-defiance (such as Dylan Thomas's challenge to death – 'Rage, rage against the dying of the light.'). But anyone who has not felt the chill in their bones of its ultimate nihilism is unworthy to be heard telling of a more hope-full way. Especially, a way of Providence. Since hovering at death's door and surviving with a busted heart, the Wheel of Fortune metaphysic has paid me many tempting visitations.

HELLO! – IS THERE SOMEBODY UP THERE?

'Providence' is a more sophisticated version of the 'Somebody-Up-There likes me' Big Story. The Christian Big Story is a Providence story – as are the other two great Abrahamic religions.

Sick, suffering and sentimental, in hospital I accepted the non-sale of Mt Vic as a work of Providence. Home, still exceedingly ill, I recognised the irrationality and wishful thinking of that view. So I needed to do some very tough reflecting. And after what I had been – and was still – going through, this was not theoretical. But where did it all fit – if it did – into Providence. Into the oversight of a caring God? I think I could just about write a (boring) book about my reflections but I will be as brief and to the point as possible.

In the Christian Big Story, God is the source of cosmic and biological evolution, and of everything in the Lifeworld. Described in the Bible and the historic creeds as *'the maker of all things visible and invisible'*. Evolution of the Lifeworld is not a mere material process. Which is why some several thousand years ago, self-conscious creatures like us emerged. Creatures able to understand how they have come to be – a process illustrated by the beautiful story of Adam and Eve.

In the New Testament, stories of Jesus' miracles – his healings of the sick, the disabled and the disturbed, and his own resurrection from the dead – are called **signs of God's Kingdom.** They are not demonstrations of power or some kind of proof of Jesus' teachings. He explicitly rejects this sort of interpretation as misleadingly evil. Rather, they are signs of the Age-To-Come. 'Thy kingdom come' is what Jesus tells his disciples to pray.

This Age-To-Come is when God will free the Lifeworld from its fallenness, its bondage to decay and suffering. Suffusing it instead with an unimaginable blessedness. Poetically described by Paul in Romans as 'Glory' (Divine luminosity or splendour). On this view, Creation's current state of evil, decay and suffering – of which wars and famines, rapes, child massacres, lies, heart attacks and universal death are a part – derives from its fallen condition. Pictured in the Bible's story of Adam and Eve as expulsion from paradise. Understood as being intentionally subjected to futility, as Paul says in chapter 8 of his letter to the Romans:

> *I consider that the sufferings of this present time are not worth comparing with the glory about*

> to be revealed to us. For the creation waits with eager longing for the revealing of the children of God; for the creation was subjected to futility, not of its own will but by the will of the one who subjected it, in hope that the creation itself will be set free from its bondage to decay and will obtain the freedom of the glory of the children of God. We know that the whole creation has been groaning in labour pains until now; and not only the creation, but we ourselves, who have the first fruits of the Spirit, groan inwardly while we wait for adoption, the redemption of our bodies. For in hope we were saved. Now hope that is seen is not hope. For who hopes for what is seen? But if we hope for what we do not see, we wait for it with patience.
>
> Likewise the Spirit helps us in our weakness; for we do not know how to pray as we ought, but that very Spirit intercedes with sighs too deep for words. And God, who searches the heart, knows what is the mind of the Spirit, because the Spirit intercedes for the saints according to the will of God.

I count myself *one of those children of God who does not know how to pray as he ought*. But meditating long and hard on all this, a little bit of light – not much – did appear. I came to see how it need not be mere emotional wish-fulfilment to view as providential my survival of the aneurysm or the non-sale of the Mt Vic house. To see these 'blessings' as tiny buds of the love and goodness that will flower fully in the Age-To-Come.

And to see, conversely, my blocked artery, heart attack, physical incapacity and medical mistakes as the consequence of inhabiting a Lifeworld that is 'subjected to futility' (but in hope not despair).

Admittedly – just like the Lotto Big Story – this Somebody-Up-There-Cares Big Story is a **reading into** personal experience a contestable, unprovable, metaphysical Big Story. A **reading into** of the Christian Big Story. A story that says at core – ontologically, its Ground of Being – the Lifeworld is personal, spiritual and caring. Promising a future restoration not only of its self-conscious, reasoning, human creatures, but also of everything else, including cats and sparrows, forests and coral reefs. When – in the words of that great mystic, Mother Julian of Norwich – 'All shall be well and all manner of thing shall be well'. Salvation by what Dante calls 'The love that moves the sun and all the other stars'.

ALL THINGS WEIRD AND THE WONDERFUL

When I was eight years-old, I had a number of decayed, first teeth extracted at the same time. The dentist administered 'laughing gas' (nitrous oxide) as the anaesthetic. Serendipitous with the future direction of my life, I underwent a thrilling, mysterious, altered-consciousness experience of racing through enormous, vaulting ancient stone churches – church after church after church, each different. Racing, racing and racing through, endlessly. To my confident recollection, I had never been inside similar churches and hadn't seen any pictures like them either. This is why, to this day, it all remains so vivid in my memory.

It was about the most amazing experience of my childhood. I told my mother about these dreams or, as I would later call them 'hallucinations'. She said, 'It's just the anaesthetic'.

I have already mentioned some strange experiences I had after the big surgery – floating on a Sea of Death and a 'vision' of God as an infinite block of concrete. But recovering at home, these two – and another, more strange still – kept demanding attention. I name them the weird and the wonderful, and they are. Maybe they, too, are 'just the anaesthetic'. But a lifetime after the extraction of my baby teeth, I am not prepared to quickly tame them as 'just the anaesthetic'. And these were experiences I had **after**, not during, the anaesthesia.

The problem with any so-called altered states of consciousness – whether induced by anaesthetics during surgery, or by other drugs, or by prayer, or by meditation, or by extreme and unusual experiences – is that what is 'seen' or 'heard' is very individualistic and its reality uncertain. Is its metaphysical status higher than everyday-life consciousness (indicative of a richer reality) or lower (indicative of crazy imaginings)?

The problem with 'normal' everyday consciousness is that what is 'seen' is corporate and pre-conditioned and so its reality may only consist in shallow consensual conformity. A consciousness of 'keeping up mentally with the Joneses'. Or – more likely, in our current cultural climate – a 'keeping up with the mentality of the scientific-materialist Joneses' – the metaphysics of the front of one's nose reality. Death destroys intersubjectivity; the intersubjectivity that makes the everyday seem the most real, whether it is or not.

On June 12, 2008 – forty-five days after open-heart surgery – I began trying to make sense of the confusing states of consciousness I experienced during the depths of my heart troubles.

Post-operatively, I sensed already some kind of creative, meaningful upheaval of both my spiritual life and my understanding of God. I didn't think God had changed, but I knew I had. Would never be quite the same spiritually again! But how? Why? There was a weirdness I needed to understand. Unsurprisingly, God the Infinite Block of Concrete came first.

WHEN GOD BECAME A BLOCK OF CONCRETE

As mentioned in Part One, trying to pray, I saw the image of the infinite block of concrete in my mind's eye (as much as one can 'see' the infinite) two or three days after exiting the ICU, whilst still terribly ill in Westmead Hospital cardiac observation ward. 'Yes', I was taking strong painkillers. 'No', my mind was not addled, I was thinking very clearly and have sharp memories of what happened. In memory I can still today 'see' that vision.

In my theologically trained mind – I felt that telling anyone about it would be as embarrassing as being discovered nude at the local shopping mall on a Saturday morning. God – an infinite block of benign concrete! Crazy stuff!

When it happened – there I was, floating on the sea of death, asking in my mind - 'What should I pray for myself?' My brain abuzz with emotional answers – 'God, heal me now'; 'Lord, guide my doctors'; 'I'm ready to go, take me'; 'What is this all about?; Why, God?'; 'I deserve this! No I don't deserve this!'; 'Why would you be concerned about an old bloke like me?'; 'What right have I to ask for your special help?'

As previously mentioned, these emotional prayers seem shallow and childish, as if I am a little boy calling on Sigmund Freud's fantasy Sky-Father. But that's just it, I *am* feeling like a little boy. A tiny, impotent, insignificant speck in a huge, overwhelming macrocosm. Then out of the blue – I experience myself praying to a benign, infinite block of concrete. Rationally it comes as shock and confusion. Emotionally and spiritually it comes as comfort and release from tension. I just let go. I feel safe.

Trying to sort it out in my head, this is part of what I scribbled on June 12th 2008:

What Did I See?

I saw that God is, the isness of everything. As I wrote that, I thought – what a weird way of saying it, too abstract.

It would be better to say that I realised that God just is and that what we must learn is how to relate to that isness. Another way of saying this, and I am finding it hard to say it in any way, is that you can't manipulate God, not by anything, including fervent prayer. But I also saw that God is totally benign and that when we relate to God we discover that benignity.

Here, I am starting to 'get it'. It has taken extended dangling on the brink of death to do it. But for the first time in my life, I admit, not just in my mind – that has always been easy – **but existentially, emotionally, to the depths of my being,** that I am not in control of my life and never ever have been. It is a lot more than an *'admit'*. More than a rationalistic nod. Rather, it is the renunciation of a fantasy and a **surrender** to the truth. A fundamental spiritual truth. In the depths of our being, we must align to God, not foolishly try to make God align to us. God is the isness of everything, and we are but fragile, mortal contingent creatures.

Writing **What Did I See?** made me realise that the Sea of Death and the concrete block were part of the same 'vision'...

... rather I occupied, was slotted into, huge, vast spaces, including a heaving grey sea. There was nothing to fear. Awe is not the right word to describe my response – rather something like gravitas. This was something like Patrick White's 'necessity'. First of all, you need to accept it, just accept. This too was God – this vastness producing a sense of gravitas.

The Australian Nobel Laureate Patrick White's saying that 'you can't accept God until you accept necessity' had both intrigued and puzzled me for a very long time. Now to my innards, I knew what he meant. I the adult now felt overwhelmingly, too, the truth of Jesus' saying *'Unless you become as a little child you cannot enter the Kingdom of God'*. He was **not** talking about the childish infantilism Sigmund Freud exploited in support of his atheism.

Oh yes! We make some choices along the way – this job or that, this partner or that – but overwhelmingly we are driven by forces outside our control. Cosmic, biological, historical, economic, cultural, social forces. And birth, maturation, ageing and lastly – inevitable death. Being in control of one's life is an absurd but captivating, bewitching modern fantasy. A fantasy cultivated in our consumer society by psychologically trained marketeers manipulating our desires in order to sell us everything from trophy-destination tours to tattoos and mobile phones. Absurdly, we believe conforming to these fashions expresses our free individuality. Sticking to such fantasies will eventually bring us undone. Hard reality will reveal what little control and individual self we possess. Floating on the sea of death definitely does it. In my case, blessedly.

God the infinite block of concrete 'said' to me - *'There is only one way - you must align your life to God, not expect God to align to you.* Do that, and become fully alive; do the opposite and waste away.

Jesus – From The Sermon On The Mount

'Therefore I tell you, do not worry about your life, what you will eat or what you will drink, or about your body, what you will wear. Is not life more than food, and the body more than clothing? Look at the birds of the air; they neither sow nor reap nor gather into barns, and yet your heavenly Father feeds them. Are you not of more value than they? And can any of you by worrying add a single hour to your span of life? And why do you worry about clothing? Consider the lilies of the field, how they grow; they neither toil nor spin, yet I tell you, even Solomon in all his glory was not clothed like one of these. But if God so clothes the grass of the field, which is alive today and tomorrow is thrown into the oven, will he not much more clothe you – you of little faith? Therefore do not worry, saying, 'What will we eat?' or 'What will we drink?' or 'What will we wear?' For it is the Gentiles who strive for all these things; and indeed your heavenly Father knows that you need all these things. But strive first for the kingdom of God and his righteousness, and all these things will be given to you as well.

> So do not worry about tomorrow, for tomorrow will bring worries of its own. Today's trouble is enough for today.'

YHWH

Having made some sense of the concrete block, about eighteen months further down the track, I was at last able to get over my embarrassment, come out of the spiritual closet, and speak to intimate friends about it.

For years, I've met annually with four male mates at a remote homestead beside the Goobragandra River in the NSW Snowy Mountains. We relish our annual rendezvous for good food, good wine, deep and desultory conversation. In late 2009, I managed to tell the 'Goobra Gang' about the time 'When God Became A Block Of Concrete'. Later, on my 70th birthday in August 2012, intriguingly, I received an extremely weighty postage parcel. It contained a concrete cube – weighing a few kilos – cast by Wayne Hooper, one of the Goobra mates. On one surface he'd etched **YHWH** (the Tetragrammaton) and on another '**I Am**'.

The Tetragrammaton (rendered in English YHWH) is the consonants-only, unpronounceable, revered name for God in the Hebrew Bible. '**I Am That I Am**' – perhaps more accurately translated from Hebrew as '**I Will Be Who I Will Be**' – is the answer God gave Moses when he asked - in the story of The Burning Bush – 'Who Are You?'. This birthday gift was witty, but more so – it was exceedingly perceptive.

At the time of the Sea of Death and God as a Concrete Block experiences, I had an even more embarrassing vision. As

I write, to this day I've not even discussed it with my intimate friends, though they will now be able to read about it here.

THE POWER OF NOTHINGNESS

As another part of *What Did I See?* I wrote this:

Yet down here – and somehow, I can't explain it, it was a down here place, there were threatening ghostly things. I never saw them because they only come if your spirit calls them but I sensed their presence – distractive/destruction in itself. The sense was palpable but they were unreal, unreality itself. Like Satan or the Devil – the Not God, therefore Nothing, No Being. I could feel about the Not Things that the prayers of living souls, my family, intimates, fellow church members, were engaging them in battle. I know this is more superstitious sounding than what I have written so far but I cannot find any other way of saying what I experienced. This was, in old-fashioned terms, angels and demons territory.

I headed this verbal outpouring '**What did I see?**' because I felt my wrestle with myself, my illness and with death gifted me with new insights and visions. But what I wrote about here feels uncomfortably superstitious and mediaeval. Most alarming.

It was directly experiential. Not just mental-thinking, or playing with abstract ideas, but an inner-seeing, visionary, palpable experience. I mean that simply as descriptive, not trying to somehow justify it. Well and truly outside the range of the normal for me. Trying to make sense of it all leaves me groping for words here, in *What did I see?* Of all that happened during this period, nothing seemed more profound and nothing was more bewildering than this. It took more than these **What did I see?** sentences to riddle order from chaos. For that, I had to draw on my wider knowledge and life experience.

The '*down here place*' was certainly not a spatial reference. It refers to dimensions of consciousness. I can only explain it as being far below the self-awareness of the 'normal' consciousness of everyday life. More like – but not the same as – the consciousness that inhabits us in dreams, nightmares, hallucinations and – differently again – in prayer and meditation.

I am wary of thinking of it as Carl Jung's notion of 'the collective unconscious'. I find him a bit too mystical and superstitious. Wary also of thinking in terms of Freud's 'unconscious'. I find him too materialist and rationalistic. But both these great ones do actually grapple with the dimensions of consciousness I am trying to understand here. Both treat it as significant for human understanding. Both delivered new insights. The current trend – shaped by so-called 'scientific' materialism – is to dismissively reduce all non-everyday experiences to nothing more than (abnormal) chemical and electrical activity in our brains. When you consider that all human understanding – including definitions of 'normal' and 'abnormal' – is bound up with electrical and chemical activity in the brain this is no help at all.

Augustine of Hippo (354-430 AD) is often referred to as either the last of the great ancient thinkers or the first of the great moderns. Except for some new terminology, there is nothing much that pioneer thinkers of the modern world, such as Freud or Jung could teach Augustine. You cannot understand the culture of Western civilisation apart from Augustine. So great has been his influence. Some of the strange or unusual words I've used in this emotional scribbling – *'threatening ghostly things'*, *'the Not God'*, *'the Not Things'*, *'Satan or the Devil'* – would make good sense to Augustine of Hippo. Only by drawing on my knowledge of him am I able to make good sense of my seemingly medieval vision.

Evil, according to Saint Augustine, is the absence of the good. This is what I am dredging up in my mind, trying to put words to this weird visionary experience. Desperately ill, at the edge of death, I say that I've experienced *'ghostly things'*. But, like evil, they come into being only if I invoke them (*'they only come if your spirit calls them'*). They are the epitome of *'destruction in itself'* but they are *'unreality itself'*. Just as Satan is *'the Not God'*, *'the Non-Being'*, these are *'the Not Things.'*

In my Augustinian understanding, God is Being and God is the Good. Evil is the absence of Being and the absence of the Good. A vast, destructive negative power. Ultimately, the power of nothingness.

In the Bible, this is sometimes expressed by vivid, concrete, apocalyptic imagery. For example, in the Book of Revelation, the Devil – God's chief opponent – is hurled into a lake of fire and sulphur to undergo torment and destruction 'forever and ever'.

In a letter to the early Christians in Corinth, St Paul gives us another take on the same ideas. Jesus, by his resurrection from the dead, he says, has entered the Age-To-Come already. This is the concrete signal of the ultimate end of death itself – the last enemy. Death – as not just as a mental concept, but as the actual power of negation. Death – *'the last enemy' shall be destroyed and God will be 'all in all'* – he says. In more abstract words (by no means necessarily the best words) – Non-Being will be subsumed by Being, Evil by the Good, Death by Life, Satan (the Adversary) by God.

Difficult though it is to find appropriate words – and to simplify these complex issues – none of this talk of God and the Devil, of Being and Nothingness, of Good and Evil is mere theory but real experience.

My sick bed visions deepened the reality of it for me in direct experiential, semi-hallucinatory ways. It sounds medieval because in a sense it is. The medieval world, albeit often superstitiously, was well aware of these deep dimensions of the Lifeworld. Whitehead's 'Fallacy of Misplaced Concreteness'– limiting reality to scientific models of the matter-energy world -blocks them out. It does not eliminate them. And blocking creates great loss and much danger. Ignoring the power of nothingness – Satan and evil – magnifies its potential for destruction. All who've experienced anything of the gamut of worldly afflictions - family violence, war, depression, despair, grief, addiction, desolation, hate, revenge, starvation, torture, exile – know this. And who hasn't?

Then there was prayer – *'I could feel about the Not Things that the prayers of living souls, my family, intimates, fellow church members, were engaging them in battle.'* In some profound way – Jung might explain it in terms of his 'collective unconscious' – I was aware of intimate bonding with others and of their prayers strengthening me against the danger of falling into the enormous negative power and nothingness of the Not God of Non-Being.

From bosons to galaxies, we view the matter-energy 'universe' as interconnected. Weirdly, in the case of Quantum Mechanics. Similarly, in this vision I experienced our human interconnectedness in God – our spirits together in the Creator Spirit. Sunday by Sunday at church, Christians recite the creed saying 'We believe… in the Communion of Saints' i.e. in the interconnectedness of all worshippers of the Most High, all Jesus' disciples, the living and the dead. This was the deepest comprehension of prayer I have ever had.

IS THERE A REASON?

After all this rather deep stuff, I was still left with a very important question – is there any reason why I am still alive? At any other time in history, anyone suffering a pseudo-aneurysm of the heart's left ventricle would be dead. The diagnosis made only post-mortem. Even in modern times, death is the most likely outcome. Inevitably then I asked and kept on asking – why am I alive? Is there a deeper purpose to my survival than happy coincidence and medical science? Wary of inventing meaning, this was a hard question to answer. This is the last bit of **What did I see?**

In the vastness of death I did not fight for life i.e. the life of the world to which I was now linked by the flimsiest thread. At no time did I struggle to live in that sense. After I had 'come back', but not articulated until I left hospital, I recognised and said 'I fought for love not life'. If love meant death, then that was OK too. *As it turned out love meant life. And now 12-06-08 I am wrestling with what that means… Writing this marks my first proper conscious recognition that this is central to whatever I am now! And key to what I saw was 'Compassion'.*

When you've been near to death but haven't died, when you've 'come back' feeling guilty about the enormous sum spent to save the old bloke that is you – you can't help asking 'what now?'

Some friends of a simple piety are keen to assure me that God must have a purpose in saving me. Though they probably have some particular project or mission in mind – and though I see their view as spiritually naïve – at the deepest level I actually agree. That purpose I say is to love. Through the afflictions of illness and the dance with death, I feel I have learnt a new level of compassion. Only God and others will tell from my behaviour if that is true or not.

DEFIBRILLATED - STRUCK BY LIGHTNING FROM THE INSIDE

Here seems to be an appropriate place in my story to recount a couple of the 'doings' of my Implanted Cardioverter Defibrillator (Defib, for short). You recall that Dr Lloyd Davis would not agree to my discharge from hospital until this was implanted. He proved very wise. Without my 'Guardian Angel', I would not be writing this small book. Since it was implanted, it has saved my life many times. My frequent deaths and resurrections, as I like to joke. I have a basic, layperson's understanding of how it works.

Pacing is the first line of defence against deadly Ventricular Fibrillation - the useless, non-pumping fluttering of the lower heart. VF starts as Ventricular Tachycardia (VT). VT is a very fast beating heart - say 150 or 200+ beats per minute. When tachycardia is first detected, the defib - in simple terms - creates a matching electrical pulse and then slows that pulse down, bringing the racing heart down with it. My defib is set to pace if my heart rate exceeds 160 beats per minute (bpm). Age plus the type of medication one is taking determines the appropriate bpm setting. My machine has paced me many times. I can't say how many times because I have not kept an accurate record. Many have happened to me unawares, either because of their short duration or because I was asleep. The latter only show up when the defib data is downloaded at the six-monthly interrogations.

A few times, because the matching-beats fix-up failed, pacing was repeated several times. This feels like you've got an electric razor buzzing on and off inside your chest. On other occasions, feeling I was starting to faint, suddenly I felt a slight rumbling sensation inside my chest and the faint feeling went away. If pacing fails to correct the arrhythmia the next treatment is electric shock. And I certainly do remember, each of the eight occasions I have been 'shocked', or as I much prefer to say more colloquially – 'zapped'.

At a press conference after the media mogul, Kerry Packer's life was saved by a defibrillator, he was famously reported to say to a journalist: *'I've been to the other side and let me tell you, son, there's fucking nothing there... there's no one waiting there for you, there's no one to judge you so you can do what you bloody well like'.* My favourite atheist, the broadcaster Phillip Adams, frequently cites this as if it somehow supports his own scepticism. Though to be fair to Adams, he cites it with a chuckle in his voice, indicating that he doesn't place much weight on Packer's theological acumen – but loves his larrikinism. In reality, Packer had no more been to the 'other side' – whatever metaphysically he might have meant by that term– than I have. And I've had eight zaps back from the edge of certain death!

Sunday after Sunday, at worship services all over the globe, Christians say these words about Jesus from the Nicene Creed: '... *For our sake he was crucified under Pontius Pilate; he suffered death and was buried. On the third day he rose again...*' A statement that summarises the New Testament Gospel story of Jesus.

To use Packer's loose terminology – Jesus is said to have gone to the 'other side' dead and buried (for three days), then come back from the 'other side' to 'this side' once more (rose again). Again, sticking with Packer's terminology, far from reporting 'nothing there', the Jesus of the resurrection narratives 'comes back from the other side' proclaiming forgiveness for his murderers – not revenge – and God's peace and love for all. This is about as far from Packer's metaphysic, and his narcissistic, nihilistic ethic - '... you can do what you bloody well like' – as might be imagined.

I have not in any sense been to the 'other side'. All I am able to report about – when hit by severe Ventricular Fibrillation – is what it is actually like to be in the throes of dying and be saved by an algorithm-coded defibrillator zap.

The eight zaps I've experienced have been spread across the years since May 2008 when my first defibrillator was implanted. The defib manufacturer's booklet describes the experience of a zap as 'a kick in the chest'. I have seen it described more colourfully as 'like being kicked in the chest by a donkey'. From the beginning, I was extremely nervous about being zapped.

I attend weekly cardiac rehabilitation sessions at my local hospital. It is common for the cardiac nurse, or even one of the local cardiologists, to refer new defibrillator recipients to me to talk about my experience. They, too, are always nervous about being zapped – about what it will feel like, whether there will be warnings. I explain that I can only say what it has been like for me.

It's like getting struck by lightning from the inside is my best shot at explaining it. The kick goes from the inside out, not – as would a donkey kick – from the outside in. Sometimes there is no warning at all. Just like the proverbial 'bolt from the blue'. Feeling faint seconds before the shock, or starting to stumble and fall, or sensing the buzz of repeated pacings, are the only warnings I have had. There is a powerful 'bang' in the chest. It feels like a sudden powerful but brief electric shock (which it is).

I don't know if the 'bang' is audible to others. I do know that these days any sharp, loud sound – a car backfire or a saucepan dropped on our slate kitchen floor – sends me into emotional panic. Feeling I have just been zapped. Zaps are welcome as salvation from sudden death. But they are, nevertheless, extremely unpleasant. I try to avoid them by adhering strictly to my rhythm-control medication regime and by avoiding excessive physical exertion.

WITNESS TO A ZAPPING

Since we discovered that we lived in the same street and renewed our old friendship, one afternoon a fortnight John Leaney and I meet for desultory conversation about matters personal, familial, political, ethical, philosophical, theological, spiritual and so on. You recall that our common near-death experiences deepened our mutual friendship and understanding.

John is the only person to witness me getting zapped. Thinking it would be helpful, he wrote up this account for me:

> *You (Bruce) and I (John) were sitting on lounges, facing each other across the coffee table. We were talking about violence in the Old Testament, and the connection with the God of love. I was waiting for your response to my comment on the matter, and distinctly remember thinking that you looked distracted. You then said 'I'm being paced', quickly followed by 'I'm going to be zapped'...you then threw up both hands, and leant back. Your eyes roll back into your head. After a few seconds, your eyes came back, and you started breathing through your mouth, making a gurgling sound, with your tongue out.*
>
> *I got up and walked over to you, and you took your glasses off and said 'where am I?' I think I said something inane like 'you're in the lounge room'.*
>
> *At this stage, you looked confused, but you were breathing normally.*

> *You looked as though you're about to stand up and I said 'please don't stand up'. You still looked as though you're about to stand up, and I put my hand on your shoulder to restrain you. You said 'please don't stop me' and I took my hand off and you sat there.*
>
> *You then put your glasses on and started to look 'normal', and you recalled that you had been zapped. The whole episode took about 25-40 seconds.*

My life had been saved again by my Guardian Angel!

One earlier episode of being zapped opened up a whole world of metaphysical questions about the real and the unreal.

It began early one Saturday morning while I was still in bed asleep. After experiencing a vivid dream that I was dying, I awoke, startled. Literally shaking my head from side to side, as a way of trying to assure myself of the accustomed reality of my bedroom. Dreams about dying are not uncommon. This one was especially scary. It felt as if I was slipping down into an abyss: much like the experience I had on the night of my heart attack. This time not in the shape of mental images and emotional feelings but as dream reality.

When you are in it, dream reality appears to have the same metaphysical status as waking reality. It is only after the dream is over that we attribute to the waking state a higher reality status than the dream state. Dismissively saying 'it was only a dream'. (Peculiarly, in modern secular culture it is usual to grant the dream world little or no reality at all. To find some way of explaining away its metaphysical status in waking – so-called 'scientific' - reality terms.) On this occasion, it began to enter my waking mind that maybe the dying in this dream was reality itself. That I was actually dying and, during sleep, unawares to waking consciousness, my defibrillator had zapped me back to life. There was a clue. But like a good detective story there is a complicated plot before the villain is unmasked.

I had acquired a new heart complication. Another *Whew! Whammy!* – as I called such occurrences in **Kickstart**. This one is named Atrial Fibrillation – AF. With AF, the two upper chambers of the heart – the atria – fibrillate or flutter. As with VF of the lower two chambers, it's an electrical problem. Quite common among older people who often have it unawares (14% of over 80s in the USA have AF). It doesn't have the immediate deadly danger of VF. But AF greatly reduces the heart's efficiency, causing fatigue. Most seriously, you are prone to blood clots forming in the heart and leading to stroke. (Why now I must take the blood thinner Warfarin, famously the main ingredient in rat poison.)

Due to the clot-danger, every attempt is made to restore normal heart rhythm (known as Sinus Rhythm). Achieved through medication or, more drastically, by electrical Cardioversion (i.e. under anaesthetic applying an electric shock to the heart). John England advised against Cardioversion for me, saying any benefit – given my crazy electricals – would be temporary. Instead, I was treated with a medication that slows the rapidity of the atria beats but does not correct their irregularity. Back to the dream and the clue.

On the Saturday of the dream, in very bold letters, I wrote in my diary - '**6.30 DYING THEN SINUS R??**' Then the day after the dream, preparing for my morning shower, I became aware that my heart was beating regularly in Sinus Rhythm - 'bdum, bdum, bdum, bdum, bdum'. And not in the irregular beats of AF - 'bb, dum, b, dum, bdum, bd, bb, bdum'. Why? My theory was that my defibrillator had in fact zapped me during sleep. Effectively giving me electrical cardioversion. And that the dream was about an actual experience of dying. But how could I be sure?

I could be certain that the sinus rhythm was real. The beats remained steady. I had new energy. Walking easily up a nearby steep hill that had been impossible since my AF began. I became more certain when after four days my permanent AF resumed.

My defibrillator, I was now convinced in my mind, had given me the equivalent of an operating-theatre executed cardioversion and, just as John England predicted, the benefit was temporary. All this was confirmed four months later when my device was interrogated. The computer-download showed that I had been zapped at 6.30 am on the very same Saturday as recorded in my diary.

My mechanical, electrical, titanium, algorithmic Guardian Angel is certainly a blessing. But she can be very severe. A weird after-effect of her bringing me back to life with a zap is how unreal waking reality, and the world of everyday life, seem for a while. I insist, though, that I haven't been anywhere – certainly not to some 'other side'. But almost leaving 'here' makes accustomed 'here', and accustomed 'me', seem very different. Sensing not just a contingent but also an abridged reality. I count this, too, a blessing from my heart attack.

COMFORT AND STRENGTH INAFFLICTION

On the eve of my 50-50 dice with death, you may recall that I got to peaceful sleep while repeating the bit of this Biblical text in bold type as a mantra:
*'We do not live to ourselves, and we do not die to ourselves. **If we live, we live to the Lord, and if we die, we die to the Lord;** so then, whether we live or whether we die, we are the Lord's. For to this end Christ died and lived again, so that he might be Lord of both the dead and the living.'*

In this final part of my story, I wrestle with my imaginary, internal critics. Those who want to mock me for my shallow or sentimental use of the mantra. Who question the validity of the comfort and strength I derived from it. Not least among them is the great British philosopher Bertrand Russell. More personally, I am trying to make sense to myself of why it was so important to me that night. And why it had the effect it did.

In Part One, I mentioned my close familiarity with **THE TEXT**, through frequently reciting it when conducting funeral services according to the Anglican rite. It's taken from the sixth book of the New Testament, the Epistle (Letter) of Paul to the Romans - 14:7-9. This was written in 55 or 56 A.D. I had to master Romans – a complex book – in the original Greek for my undergraduate degree in theology. The translation I've used here is the *New Revised Standard Version* (NRSV).

In June 2008, I wrote this about the mantra- emotional, rough, convoluted and unaltered:

I lived not in the mere words of this text – some sort of superstructure – but in its dug foundation. A sense of absolute abandonment. Not to a blind fate. Not to some super-daddy or human projected ego either. To the foundational reality that what had brought me to being – the whole billion of years cosmos, humanity, animality, sociality had been good/kind (what word) in bringing me to be and there was nothing else but to abandon myself to that Creatorate. CREATORATE.

This was what Christ did – that is why Christ is the clue to God, not the other way round.

We are the Lord's – simple as that, we are not our own, never have been, never will be except by gift. For a while, before we realise we are not our own, we think we are, act like that and there is no sense of gift, only the horror (espec. with death) of realising we are not our own, horror because no gift, just trap (e.g. Bertrand Russell and blind senseless matter.)

Anyone who has ever had a child is familiar with the renewed wonderment of life that birth brings with it. If you have come back from the brink of death– whether from illness, injury or accident – you will likely experience that same renewed wonderment. My words expressing it are certainly stumbling.

NEOLOGISM

Attempting to speak about this wonderment, I've invented an awkward word. 'Creatorate' does not appear in any English dictionary. By repeating it in upper-case letters –

'CREATORATE', I immediately recognised it as a neologism. It is decidedly idiosyncratic. For me here, 'Creatorate' is the whole complex process that brings us into being as knowing and self-knowing creatures. It protests to the atheistic critics inside my head – 'Don't think I operate in some simplistic 19th century, binary Creation versus Evolution debate'. Creatorate is the whole complex process: God> Cosmic Evolution> Biological Evolution> Consciousness> Sociality> Language> Self Consciousness> Cultural history. Everything that brings us to being as we are.

How and why did THE TEXT work such wonders for me? I want to understand that! But the truly big questions rolling around in my mind are, 'Was I on solid ground or fooling myself? Can you trust the Creatorate?'

The answer can be 'Yes' or 'No'. **'Yes'** you can trust the Creatorate as benevolent and personal. **'No'** you can't trust the Creatorate because it is impersonal and hostile to the likes of us.

As I mull this over – wrestling with serious doubts – the mathematician, philosopher and Nobel laureate Bertrand Russell (died 1970) comes to mind. In my short-lived atheist days, I recall the powerful impact on me of reading his emotion-charged **'No!'**. And of how it always comes up in times of doubt to this day. A 'No!' first published in 1903 as part of the essay *A Free Man's Worship* in Esquire magazine. Republished in his 1957 book **Why I Am Not A Christian**. He wrote:

> *'Brief and powerless is Man's life; on him and all his race the slow, sure doom falls pitiless and dark. Blind to good and evil, reckless of destruction,*

omnipotent matter rolls on its relentless way; for Man, condemned today to lose his dearest, tomorrow himself to pass through the gate of darkness, it remains only to cherish, ere yet the blow falls, the lofty thoughts that ennoble his little day; disdaining the coward terrors of the slave of Fate, to worship at the shrine that his own hands have built; undismayed by the empire of chance, to preserve a mind free from the wanton tyranny that rules his outward life; proudly defiant of the irresistible forces that tolerate, for a moment, his knowledge and his condemnation, to sustain alone, a weary but unyielding Atlas, the world that his own ideals have fashioned despite the trampling march of unconscious power.'

There is nothing actually new here from a previous part of my story. Russell has opted for the Lotto Way, not the Somebody-Up-There Way. His chosen path along the Lotto Way is an heroic, humanistic, will-to-defiance path. His prose is purple, but I still find it a bit seductive. I think it's the glamour of metaphysical defiance. Eve and Adam all over again!

FAITH – NO THANK YOU!

I know people will say that my repetition of the Pauline text as a mantra was a sign of my faith. That well and truly gets up my spiritual nose, because **faith** is certainly **not** the word I would use.

Once-upon-a-time a profound biblical word, 'faith' is now a loaded term. Frequently used to describe someone taking 'a leap in the dark' or 'accepting dogmatic teachings on mere authority'. Faith has become the opposite to doubt – blind faith. 'Faith' as this binary – faith versus doubt – defines me, a Christian theist, as irrational and my doubting atheist critics (both those inside and those outside my head) as rational. As a final modern travesty, 'faith' is twisted into the simplistic matter of whether you (mentally) believe in God or not.

The word I want to put on the record, more accurately denoting use of my prayer mantra is 'Yes!' – not faith.

Put in the simplest way – Is Life ultimately for us or against us? Is it a 'Yes!'? Or is it a 'No!'? Praying the mantra affirms my answer was – and is – 'Yes'.

'Yes' – in life and through death – *If we live, we live to the Lord, and if we die, we die to the Lord; so then, whether we live or whether we die, we are the Lord's.*

'Trust' is probably an even a better word than 'Yes!' 'Yes' can still be misunderstood as just a head trip. Prior to the modern faith-doubt binary, 'trust' was the classic interpretation of what Christian thought and practice meant by 'faith in God'.

'Trust' includes the whole self. It's a 'Yes' with the will, with the emotions, with the intuition, with the spirit and with the mind. Trust is an existential stance not a mind trip, not a philosophical or intellectual game. A real 'No' is also an existential stance. A mere intellectual -in the mind only – No! is a pose.

An agnostic 'Yes-and-No' is a possible theoretical stance. But in day-to-day lived life, the life of the whole self, it is impossible. We live either Yes! Or No! – consciously or otherwise, consistently or otherwise. There is no agnostic fence to sit on when it comes to acting and not just thinking.

I lived not in the mere words of this text – some sort of superstructure – but in its dug foundation. A sense of absolute abandonment. Not to a blind fate. Not to some super-daddy or human projected ego either. To the foundational reality that what had brought me to being… this was what Christ did – that is why Christ is the clue to God, not the other way round.

Abandoning oneself to the Creatorate – saying 'Yes I trust you as benevolent and personal' – in the circumstance of dying by violent crucifixion, as Jesus did, is certainly counterintuitive. Such trust – in light of one's own and all the world's evil sufferings – in nature, in history and in face of death itself – remains just as counterintuitive as ever.

'For to this end Christ died and lived again, so that he might be Lord of both the dead and the living.'

According to the Gospel stories, Jesus was acutely aware that he would die a violent, murderous death at human hands. And that God was not going to rescue him. In some profound sense, murder was his Divine destiny. The Gospels interpret his death as both exposing the depths of human evil and also as a means of reconciling evil, sinful humanity to God. (There are a number of theories about how the latter is supposed to work. Some exceedingly profound - such as Rene Girard's modern scapegoat theory. There are others - some widely known -that are crude or plain silly. We don't need to explore any of them here.)

In the Garden of Gethsemane – with his assassins about to pounce – Jesus fervidly prays to God, asking to be delivered from their evil machinations. But as he wrestles with God – with his 'cup of death' destiny – he ends his agonised prayer saying '... *yet, not what I will, but what you will*'. This was his abandonment, not to fate but to God. Whom he called 'Father'.

Later, according to the Gospel accounts, as he was dying on the cross, he cried out in Aramaic 'Eloi, Eloi, lema sabachthani?'. In English – '*My God, My God why have you forsaken me?*' He did not curse God. Or – as did Russell – lament about destruction by '*the trampling march of unconscious power*'. He prayed to fathom the unfathomable.

In my own very tiny way, this is what I am doing as I repeat the mantra. It could be called 'counterintuitive trust'. It is not 'blind faith'. A Creatorate that brings to being a Mozart or an Einstein, a Jane Austen or a Marie Curie – or just me and you – only to cast us all into nothingness is not a 'makes-good-sense' plausible Big Story. On the contrary, it is reductionist irrationality invoking spiritual nihilism.

In Anglican churches on Easter Sunday morning, it is customary to commence worship with the priest or bishop saying 'He is risen'. The people responding, 'He is risen indeed'. At such a service in a large rural centre some years ago, I began my sermon saying, 'Adolf Hitler is risen, the Fuhrer is risen indeed'. As you may imagine, I needed to explain myself hastily, before the congregation rose up to eject me from church and town. One large-limbed cattle farmer told me afterwards that he was the blink of an eye from rushing forward to break my jaw.

The Gospels and Paul say that after his death Jesus appeared alive from heaven to his disciples. From our perspective, that is to say he appeared from the future, from the realm of God. These resurrection appearances, Paul says in **THE TEXT**, reveal Jesus as the Lord in a particular way – '*For to this end Christ died and lived again, so that he might be Lord of both the dead and the living.*'

As I've explored already, resurrection into the 'World to Come' is participation in the re-creation and restoration of the whole Lifeworld. Free from decay, evil and death. God's intended destiny for us all and for everything. It is abandonment to this life-giving, saving, loving God that filled me with peace and allowed me to sleep deeply on the eve of my heart surgery. For whether I live or whether I die, I trust that I am a beloved of the Lord God.

This is not the place to discuss the evidence for – or the metaphysical nature of – Jesus' resurrection appearances. Books abound – good and bad – discussing, 'proving', 'demonstrating', 'interpreting' the reliability of the stories about Jesus' resurrection. They are about that which I call the **WHAT** of the resurrection appearances; and that is important. But I have no wish to add to their abundance. Just to say, clearly the originator of the Lifeworld – the One who created everything from nothing - would be more than capable of a comparatively minor feat such as a resurrection. Of course, if no such originator can be imagined, then there would be no reason to expect such an unusual happening. Resurrection would have no apparent evolutionary purpose except as a human invented fantasy to keep at bay the fear of death. The **WHAT** of the resurrection appearances is as simple as that!

My interest is much more about the meaning, the **WHO**, not the **WHAT**, of Jesus' resurrection appearances. Without a meaningful context, the appearances become just one big yawn of a 'it's a miracle, so what?' The **WHO** is more compelling as a 'makes good sense,' persuasive fit', with the whole Christian Big Story. More persuasive than the many good reasons that can be amassed for the **WHAT** of the resurrection.

In the Christian Big Story, it is Jesus **WHO** is the risen one. Jesus from the nowhere village of Nazareth. Jesus the forgiver, the compassionate, the healer, the innocent sufferer, the peace-maker. Jesus the champion of women, of minorities, of outcasts. Jesus the teacher, who proclaims the love of God and the Golden Rule, gives a premium value to children and little sparrows. Jesus who commands love of enemies and non-violence. Jesus of the Gospels – the one truly good person credibly portrayed in all of literature. Jesus, murdered through the collusion of 'church' and 'state'. Jesus murdered at the behest of the people, the mob crying 'crucify him, crucify him'.

This is the one God raised from the dead.

– *that is why Christ is the clue to God, not the other way round.*

Instead of 'Jesus' as the name of the risen one, try substituting Hitler as the **WHO** – as I did that Easter morning. Or try substituting even the greatest and best – say Socrates, Florence Nightingale or Nelson Mandela. 'Jesus is risen' is the '**WHO**' that still makes-the-most -good-sense. His resurrection is the cornerstone of a building called The Christian Big Story.

Jesus was so much in God, and God in him, that he soon came to be understood as God incarnate. The deepest revelation of God beholden by human beings. A loving God. A suffering God.

Yes – a suffering God!

All the sufferings of our fallen world, including my own small afflictions as told in this story, raise deep questionings of God. That is why, in the words of Dietrich Bonhoeffer, brilliant theologian, hanged by the Gestapo at Flossenburg in 1945 for opposition to Nazism, *'Only a suffering God can help'*.

'Whether we live or whether we die, we are the Lord's.'

POSTSCRIPT

Physically, the story of my broken heart since 2008, can best be described as 'steady as she goes with slow decline'. Some of this the result, of course, of ageing, not heart disease. Best illustrated by my daily walk. Taken every day since May 2008. The maximum walk I achieved at my recovery peak in early 2010 - about eighteen months after the aneurysm repair – was 80 minutes. It has declined in steps – AF was a big downhill step - until today the maximum time I can walk is 30 minutes.

When I visit my Pharmacy, I joke about ordering either the smorgasbord or Dr England's snack pack. On most Fridays, I attend Heart Rehabilitation at Katoomba Hospital. In many ways, Rehab has been my salvation, not so much because of the gym regime, though that is good, but what I call the psychic regime.

The program is run by Adam – a specialist cardiac nurse with a huge fund of knowledge and compassion. He is always ready to answer the questions that continuously arise for those of us living with heart disease. We constantly feel – most often fallaciously – that something is going wrong again – a chest pain, fatigue, fresh palpitations, breathlessness. The full hypochondria array. Adam reassures us or points the way to help.

Metaphysically – my (other) heart is mostly in the 'as well as can be' category. That is to say, mentally and spiritually I enjoy daily the same kind of peace and joy, struggle and testing, up and down that I've written more than enough about already.

But I carry a sorrow for the spiritual heart of my own culture and country. I subscribe to the view of the great German historian Leopold von Ranke that every generation is equidistant from eternity.

The sorrow I carry for Australia in particular – and Western Culture in general – is for its increasing spiritual emptiness. Almost it seems in proportion to our expanded capacity in the physical world we have become dimwitted and crippled in the spiritual world. Many otherwise intelligent people dabble in spiritualities that are borderline superstitions, or explore the traditions of another culture whilst mocking and deriding their own. Many more have begun to espouse a shallow atheism.

I know it's a bit 'cranky-old-man' to call some of the newer generations 'fashionista atheists'. But actually, the popular culture of secular, consumer Australia is nearing the point where 'God-botherers', such as me, will be charged, like Socrates, for attempting to corrupt the youth of our democracy.

www.ingramcontent.com/pod-product-compliance
Lightning Source LLC
Chambersburg PA
CBHW052307300426
44110CB00035B/2170